My Cooking Recipe Book

Irresistible and Wallet-Friendly Recipes

Ed T. Smith

TARRAGON VINEGAR. Fill a wide-mouthed bottle with tarragon leaves, gathered on a dry day, just before the plant begins to flower. Dry the leaves a little before the fire, steep them a fortnight in the best vinegar, and strain it fine through a flannel jelly bag. Pour it into half-pint bottles, cork them up carefully, and keep them in a dry place. This forms an agreeable addition to soups and salad sauce, and to mix with mustard.

TARTAR WINE. Add to a quantity of mare's milk a sixth part of water, and pour the mixture into a wooden vessel. Use as a ferment an eighth part of sour cow's milk; but at any future preparation, a small portion of old koumiss will answer better. Cover the vessel with a thick cloth, and set it in a place of moderate warmth, leaving it at rest for twenty four hours. At the end of this time the milk will become sour, and a thick substance will be gathered on its surface. Now with a churn-staff, beat it till the thick substance just mentioned, be intimately blended with the subjacent fluid. In this situation leave it at rest for twenty four hours more. Afterwards pour it into a higher and narrower vessel, resembling a churn, where the agitation must be repeated as before, till the liquor appear to be perfectly combined. In this state it is called koumiss, the taste of which ought to be a pleasant mixture of sweet and sour. Agitation must be employed every time before it is used. This wine, prepared by the Tartars, is cooling and antiseptic. Sometimes aromatic herbs, as angelica, are infused in the liquor during fermentation.

TARTS. Sweetmeats made with syrups are formed into pies and tarts the same as raw fruits, and the same crusts may be used for them. Tarts made of any kind of jam are usually formed with a crust round the bottom of the dish, the sweetmeat is then put in, and little ornaments of crust placed over the top, made with a jagging iron. Sugar paste is suitable for these. Little tartlets are made in the same way, only baked in tins and turned out.——Take apples, or pears, cut them in small quarters, and set them over the fire, with a piece of lemon peel, and some cinnamon; let them simmer in as much water as will cover them, till tender; and if you bake them in tin pattipans, butter them first, and lay over a thin paste; lay in some sugar, then the fruit, with three or four tea-spoonfuls of the liquor they were simmered in; put in a little more sugar, and lid them over. If your tarts are made of apricots, green almonds, nectarines, or green plums, they must be scalded before you use them, and observe to put nothing to them but sugar, and as little water as possible; make use of the syrup they were scalded in, as you did for your apples, &c. Cherries, currants, raspberries, and all ripe fruits need not be scalded; and if you make your tarts in china, or glass patties, lay the sugar at bottom, then the fruit, with a little more sugar on the top; put no paste at the bottom, only lid them over, and bake them in a slack oven. You have receipts how to make crust for tarts; mince pies must be baked in tin patties, that you may slip them out into a dish, and a puff paste is the best for them. When you make sweetmeat tarts, or a crocant tart, lay in the sweetmeats, or preserved fruit either in glass or china patties that are small, for that purpose; lay a very thin crust on the top, and let them be baked no more than till your crust is nicely coloured, and that in a slow oven. If you would have a crocant tart for the middle of the table, or a side-dish, have a glass, or china dish, of what size you please, and lay in the preserved fruit of different sorts, (you must have a round cover just the size of the inside of your dish) roll out a sugar crust, the thickness of an half crown, and lay over the cover; mark it with marking irons made on purpose for that use, of what shapes you please; then put the crust, with the cover, into a very slack oven, not to discolour it, only to have it crisp. When you take it out of the oven, loosen it from the cover very gently, and when quite cold, take it carefully off, and lay over your sweetmeats, and it being hollow, you will see the fruit through it. If the tart is not eaten, only take off the lid, and your sweetmeats may be put into the pots again.

TEA. The habit of drinking tea frequently, and in large quantities, cannot fail to be injurious, as it greatly weakens and relaxes the tone of the stomach. This produces indigestion, nervous trembling and weakness, attended with a pale, wan complexion. When tea is taken only at intervals, and after solid food, it is salutary and refreshing; but when used as a substitute for plain nourishing diet, as is too commonly the case amongst the lower classes, it is highly pernicious, especially as large quantities of a spurious description are too frequently imposed upon the public. The policy which compels a very numerous class to purchase this foreign article, for procuring which immense sums are sent out of the country, while the produce of our own soil is comparatively withheld by an exorbitant system of taxation, cannot be too severely condemned, as alike injurious to health, to the interests of agriculture, and to the comfort and industry of the people. The duty on foreign tea has indeed been greatly encreased, but at the same time, so has the duty on malt and beer; no encouragement therefore is given to the home consumption, but the money which ought to be paid for the production of barley and malt is given to the foreigner, while by the enormous price of the article, a powerful stimulus is furnished for attempting an illicit importation, and for the pernicious adulteration of what is now esteemed almost a common necessary of life. It is desirable to lessen the injurious effects of tea as much as possible by mixing it with milk, which will render it softer and more nutritious. With the addition of sugar it may be made to form a wholesome breakfast for those who are strong and live freely, operating as a diluent for cleansing the bladder and kidneys, and the alimentary passages. Persons of weak nerves ought however to abstain from tea, as they would from drains and cordials, as it causes the same kind of irritation on the delicate fibres of the stomach, which ends in lowness, trembling, and vapours. Tea should never be drunk hot at any time, as it tends still more to produce that relaxation which ought to be carefully avoided. Green tea is less wholesome than black or bohea.

TEA CAKES. Rub four ounces of butter into eight ounces of flour, mix with it eight ounces of currants, and six of fine Lisbon sugar. Add two yolks and one white of eggs, and a spoonful of brandy. Roll the paste about the thickness of a biscuit, and cut it out with a wine glass into little cakes. The white of the other egg beaten up, may be washed over them, and then they may be dusted with fine sugar.

TEA-KETTLES. Hard water used for tea is apt to form an offensive crust inside the tea-kettle, which may be prevented by frequent cleaning, or putting a flat oyster shell at the bottom. This will attract the stony particles that are in the water, and the concretion will be formed upon it.

TEA-POTS. An infusion of tea is always more perfect in a metal tea-pot, than in one of stone or earthenware. If boiling water be poured into two tea-pots, one of bright silver or polished tin, and the other of black stoneware, and they be left in a room of moderate temperature, it will be found that the former will retain its heat nearly twice as long as the other. Tea-pots of polished metal are therefore to be preferred.

TEATS. Sore teats, in Neat Cattle, is an affection in those of the cow kind, to which some are much more subject than others; especially such as have newly or lately calved. When the teats of these animals are affected during the summer months, they often become ulcerated, and by the teazing of the flies, the cattle are rendered difficult to be milked; they also become a very great nuisance at the periods of milking, as the discharges from them are apt, without much attention, to pass between the fingers of the operator into the milk-pail, and spoil the milk. The affection is caused by inflammation, irritation, and too much distention of the parts by the milk. In order to the removal of it, the milk should be first frequently drawn, and the parts well washed with soft soap and warm water; after which, a substance composed of elder ointment and wax melted together, to which is then added a little alum and sugar of lead, in fine powder, may be used to the parts after milking at night and in the morning; or a weak solution of white vitriol and a little sugar of lead, in soft water may be made use of in the same way, in some cases, with more advantage. The addition of a little assafœtida, and such like substances, in powder, is, it is said, beneficial in the summer season in driving away the flies. Great care is to be taken to keep the teats as clean as possible during the time of cure.

TEETH AND GUMS. In order to preserve the teeth and gums, they require to be cleaned very carefully; for if the enamel of the teeth be worn off by an improper mode of cleaning, they will suffer more injury than by a total neglect. A common skewer of soft wood, bruised and bitten at the end, will make the best brush for this purpose. Once a week dip the skewer brush into a few grains of gunpowder, after they have been bruised, and it will remove every spot and blemish till the teeth appear beautifully white. The mouth should be well washed after the operation, to prevent any ill effects of the gunpowder. Teeth, if not regularly cleaned, are apt to contract a false kind of enamel which is injurious to the gums, leaving the fangs of the teeth bare, so that they are soon destroyed, by being exposed to the air, and for want of being protected by the gums. This tartarous enamel must therefore be scaled off, that the gums may grow up to their proper place. Raspberries or strawberries eaten plentifully have been found to dissolve these concretions, and contribute to the preservation of the teeth and gums. Tooth powders and tinctures also have their use. A very convenient powder may be made of charcoal pounded in a mortar, and sifted fine. Apply a little of it to the teeth twice a week, and it will not only render them beautifully white, but also make the breath sweet, and the gums firm and comfortable. The charcoal may be ground in water, and so preserved for use. A tincture for the gums may be made of three ounces of the tincture of bark, and half an ounce of sal ammoniac, mixed together. Dip the finger into a tea-spoonful of the tincture, and rub the gums and teeth with it, which are afterwards to be washed with warm water. This tincture not only cures the toothache, but preserves the teeth and gums, and causes them to adhere to each other.

TENANT AT SUFFERANCE. When a lease is expired, and the tenant keeps possession without any new contract, he is deemed a tenant at sufferance. But on the landlord's acceptance of any rent after the expiration of the lease, the tenant may hold the premises from year to year, till half a year's notice is given.

TENANT AT WILL. A tenant at will is one who holds an estate or tenement at the will of the landlord, and may at any time be ejected. Meanwhile he is at liberty to leave when he chooses, on giving proper notice, and cannot be compelled to occupy.

TENCH. These are a fine flavoured fresh-water fish, and should be killed and dressed as soon as caught. They abound very much in the dykes of Lincolnshire. When they are to be bought, examine whether the gills are red and hard to open, the eyes bright, and the body stiff. The tench has a slimy matter about it, the clearness and brightness of which indicate freshness. The season for this delicate fish is July, August, and September. When to be dressed, put them into cold water, boil them carefully, and serve with melted butter and soy. They are also very fine stewed, or fricasseed, as follows. To fricassee tench white. Having cleaned your tench very well, cut off their heads, slit them in two, and if large, cut each half in three pieces, if small, in two: melt some butter in a stewpan, and put in your tench; dust in some flour, and pour in some boiling water, and a few mushrooms, and season it with salt, pepper, a bundle of sweet herbs, and an onion stuck with cloves: when this boils, pour in a pint of white wine boiling hot; let it stew till sufficiently wasted; take out the fish, and strain the liquor, saving the mushrooms; bind your fricassee with the yolk of three or four eggs beaten up with a little verjuice, some parsley chopped fine, and a little nutmeg grated; stir it all the time it boils, scum it very clean, pour your sauce over the fish, and send it to table.—To fricassee tench brown. Prepare your tench as in the other receipt; put some butter and flour into a stewpan, and brown it; then put in the tench with the same seasoning you did your white fricassee; when you have tossed them up, moisten them with a little fish broth; boil a pint of white wine, and put to your fricassee, stew it till enough, and properly wasted; then take the fish up, and strain the liquor, bind it with a brown cullis, and serve it up. If asparagus or artichokes are in season, you may boil these, and add them to your fricassee.

TENCH BROTH. Clean the fish, and set them on the fire with three pints of water; add some parsley, a slice of onion, and a few peppercorns. Simmer till the fish is broken, the broth become good, and reduced one half. Add some salt, and strain it off. Tench broth is very nutricious, and light of digestion.

THICK MILK. Beat up an egg, and add to it a tea spoonful of flour. Mix it smooth with a tea-spoonful of cold milk, and put to it a pint of boiling milk. Stir it over a slow fire till it boils, then pour it out, and add a little sugar and nutmeg. The saucepan should have a little cold water put into it first, to prevent the milk from burning at the bottom, or marbles boiled in it will answer the same purpose.

THICKENED GRAVY. To a quart of gravy allow a table-spoonful of thickening, or from one to two table-spoonfuls of flour, according to the thickness required. Put a ladleful of the gravy into a basin with the thickening, stir it up quick, add the rest by degrees, till it is all well mixed. Then pour it back into a stewpan, and leave it by the side of the fire to simmer for half an hour longer, that the thickening may be thoroughly incorporated with the gravy. Let it neither be too pale nor too dark a colour. If not thick enough, let it stew longer, or add to it a little glaze or portable soup. If too thick, it may be diluted with a spoonful or too of warm broth or water.

THICKENED SOUP. Put into a small stewpan three table-spoonfuls of the fat taken off the soup, and mix it with four table-spoonfuls of flour. Pour in a ladleful of the soup, mix it with the rest by degrees, and boil it up till it is smooth. This may be rendered more savoury by adding a little ketchup. The soup should be strained through a tammis.

THICKENING. Clarified butter is best for this purpose, or put some fresh butter into a stewpan over a slow clear fire. When it is melted, add fine flour sufficient to make it the thickness of paste. Stir it well together with a wooden spoon for fifteen or twenty minutes, till it is quite smooth, and the colour of a guinea. This must be done very gradually and patiently, or it will be spoiled. Pour it into an earthen pan, and it will keep good a fortnight in summer, and longer in winter. Particular attention must be paid in making it; if it gets any burnt smell or taste, it will spoil every thing it is put into. When cold, it should be thick enough to cut out with a knife, like a solid paste. This is a very essential article in the kitchen, and the basis of consistency in most made dishes, soups, sauces, and ragouts. In making this thickening, the less butter and the more flour is used the better. They must be thoroughly worked together, and the broth or soup added by degrees. Unless well incorporated, the sauce will taste floury, and have a greasy disagreeable appearance. To prevent this, it must be finished and cleansed, after it is thickened, by adding a little broth or warm water, and setting it by the side of the fire to raise any fat that is not thoroughly incorporated with the gravy, that it may be carefully removed as it comes to the top. Some cooks merely thicken their soups and sauces with flour, or the farina of potatoe; and others use the fat skimmings off the top of broth, as a substitute for butter.

THORNS AND SPLINTERS. To run prickles or thorns, such as those of roses, thistles, and chesnuts, or little splinters of wood or bone, into the hands, feet, or legs, is a very common accident, and provided any such substance be immediately extracted, it is seldom attended with any bad consequences. But the more certain prevention is a compress of linen dipped in warm water, and applied to the part, or to bathe it a little while in warm water. If the thorn or splinter cannot be extracted directly, or if any part of it be left in, it causes an inflammation, and nothing but timely precaution will prevent its coming to an abscess. A plaster of shoemaker's wax spread upon leather, draws these wounds remarkably well. When it is known that any part of the splinter remains, an expert surgeon would open the place and take it out; but if it be unobserved, as will sometimes happen when the substance is very small, till the inflammation begins, and no advice can at once be procured, the steam of water should be applied to it first, and then a poultice of bread crumb and milk, with a few drops of peruvian balsam. It is quite necessary that the injured part should be kept in the easiest posture, and as still as possible. If this does not soon succeed, good advice must be procured without delay, as an accident of this kind neglected, or improperly treated, may be the occasion of losing a limb. In this and all other cases of inflammation, a forbearance from animal food and fermented liquors, is always advisable.

THRUSH. This disorder in children affects the mouth and throat, and sometimes the stomach. In the former case it will be sufficient to cleanse the mouth with a little sage tea, sweetened with the honey of roses, and mixed with a dram of borax. In the latter, great benefit may be derived from a decoction of carrots in water, or an ounce of linseed boiled in a pint of water till reduced to a consistence, and sweetened with two ounces of honey, a table-spoonful of which may be given occasionally. This complaint may generally be prevented by a due attention to cleanliness, daily washing and bathing the child in lukewarm water, washing its mouth after it has been applied to the breast, giving it pure air, and removing any obstruction in the bowels by the use of manna or tamarinds.

THYME. These plants may be easily raised from seed, by slipping the roots and branches, and by cuttings; but the seed method is seldom practised, except with the second sort, or garden thyme. The seed should be sown in the early spring on light, rich, dry ground, which should be properly dug over, and the surface be made moderately smooth with the spade. As the seed is small, it should not be sown too thick, or be covered too deep: the seed is best sown while the ground is fresh stirred, either broad-cast on the surface, raking it in lightly, or in flat shallow drills, earthed over thinly: the plants appear in two or three weeks. It is necessary to be careful to keep them well weeded, giving occasional light waterings in dry weather; and by June they will require thinning, especially if the plants are to grow stocky, and with bushy full heads; in which case they should be set out to six or eight inches distance; when those thinned out may be planted in another place, in rows six or eight inches asunder, giving water till fresh rooted, keeping the whole clean from weeds by occasional hoeing between them in dry days, which will also stir the surface of the earth, and much improve the growth of the plants: they will be in perfection for use in summer, or early in autumn. Some think the common thyme best cultivated for kitchen use in beds or borders, in rows at least half a foot apart, employing for the purpose either the young seedling plants, which are fit to set out, or the root slips of old plants, each of which soon increase into plants of bushy growths proper for being cropped for the above use. It may also often be well cultivated as an edging to herbary and other compartments; in both of which methods the plants multiply exceedingly fast by offsets, and are abiding, furnishing the means of great future increase. Some should, however, always be annually raised from seed in the above manner, as such plants possess a stronger aromatic quality than those from old ones. When it is intended to increase any particular varieties, and continue them the same with certainty, it can only be effected by slips and cuttings. In respect to the offsets and slips, all the sorts multiply by offsets of the root and slips of the branches: the rooted slips are the most expeditious method, as the old plants increase into many offset stems rising from the root, each furnished with fibres; and by taking up the old plants in the spring, &c. and slipping or dividing them into separate parts, not too small, with roots to each, and planting them in beds of good earth, in rows half a foot asunder, giving water directly, and repeating it occasionally in dry weather till they have taken root, and begin to shoot at top; they soon grow freely, and form good bushy plants in two or three months. The strong slips of the branches without roots, succeed when planted any time in the early spring season in a shady border, in rows four or five inches distant, giving due waterings; and become good plants by autumn, when they may be planted out where they are to remain. The cuttings of the young branches grow readily, the same as the slips, when planted at the same season in a shady place, and well watered. The common thyme is in universal use as a pot-herb for various culinary purposes; it may also be employed in assemblage with other small plants, to embellish the fronts of flower-borders, shrubbery clumps, small and sloping banks, &c. placing the plants detached or singly, to form little bushy tufts, and in which the variegated sorts, and the silver thyme and lemon thyme particularly, form a very agreeable variety. The lemon thyme is also in much estimation for its peculiar odoriferous smell. Some of each of these sorts may also be potted, in order to be moved occasionally to any particular places as may be required, and under occasional shelter in severe winters, to preserve the plants more effectually in a lively state; likewise some of the mastick thyme. Spanish and Portugal thymes are also sometimes potted for the same purpose, and to place under the protection of a garden frame or greenhouse in winter, to continue them in a more fresh and lively growth; and sometimes some of the smaller thymes are sown or planted for edgings to particular beds or borders for variety, such as the lemon thyme, silver-leaved and variegated sorts; also occasionally the common thyme; and all kept low, close and regular, by clipping them at the sides and tops annually in the summer season. All the several sorts and varieties possess an aromatic quality, which principally resides in the leaves, whence it is imparted and affords a line agreeable fragrance. But the first three kinds are much the most noted and valued in kitchen gardens, and more especially the common thyme, which is so very useful as a culinary herb.

TIN COVERS. Properly to clean tin covers and pewter pots, get the finest whiting, which is only sold in large cakes, the small being mixed with sand. Powder and mix a little of it with a drop of sweet oil, rub the pots and covers well with it, and wipe them clean. Then dust over some dry whiting in a muslin bag, and rub the articles bright with dry leather. The last is to prevent rust, which must be carefully guarded against by wiping thoroughly dry, and setting them by the fire when they come from table. If covers are once hung up without wiping, the steam will be sure to rust the inside.

TINCTURE OF ALLSPICE. Bruise three ounces of allspice, and steep it in a quart of brandy. Shake it up occasionally and after a fortnight pour off the clear liquor. It makes a most grateful addition in all cases where allspice is used, in gravies, or to flavour and preserve potted meats.

TINCTURE OF BARK. To make the compound tincture, take two ounces of Peruvian bark powdered, half an ounce of Seville orange peel, and half an ounce of bruised cinnamon. Infuse the whole in a pint and a half of brandy, let it stand five or six days in a close vessel, and then strain off the tincture. Take one or two tea-spoonfuls twice a day in any suitable liquor, sharpened with a few drops of the spirits of vitriol. This tincture is highly beneficial in intermitting fevers, and in slow, nervous, or putrid fevers, especially towards their decline.

TINCTURE OF CINNAMON. This exhilirating cordial is made by pouring a bottle of the best brandy on three ounces of bruised cinnamon. A tea-spoonful of it, and a lump of sugar, in a glass of good sherry or madeira, with the yolk of an egg beaten up in it, was formerly considered as the balsam of life. Two tea-spoonfuls of it in a wine glass of water, are at present a very pleasant remedy in nervous languors, and in relaxations of the bowels. In the latter case, five drops of laudanum may be added to each dose.

TINCTURE OF CLOVES. Bruise three ounces of cloves, steep them for ten days in a quart of brandy, and strain off the tincture through a flannel sieve. It imparts an excellent flavour to mulled wine. In all cases tinctures are to be preferred to essences, as affording a much finer flavour.

TINCTURE OF LEMON PEEL. A very easy and economical way of obtaining and preserving the flavour of lemon peel, is to fill a wide-mouthed pint bottle half full of brandy or rum; and when a lemon is used, pare off the rind very thin, and put it into the spirits. In the course of a fortnight the liquor will be strongly flavoured with the lemon.

TINCTURE OF NUTMEG. Steep three ounces of nutmeg in a quart of brandy, and let it stand a fortnight. Shake it up occasionally, and then pour off the clear liquor.

TINCTURE OF RHUBARB. Take two ounces and a half of rhubarb, and half an ounce of lesser cardamon seeds; steep them for a week in a quart of brandy, and strain off the tincture. To make the bitter tincture of rhubarb, add an ounce of gentian root, and a dram of snake root. The tincture is of great use in case of indigestion, pain or weakness of the stomach; and from one to three or four spoonfuls may be taken every day.

TINGEING OF GLASS. The art of tingeing glass of various colours is by mixing with it, while in a state of fusion, some of the metallic oxides; and on this process, well conducted, depends the formation of pastes. Blue glass is formed by means of oxide of cobalt; green, by the oxide of iron or copper; violet, by oxide of manganese; red, by a mixture of the oxides of copper and iron; purple, by the purple oxide of gold; white, by the oxides of arsenic and of zinc; yellow, by the oxide of silver, and by combustible bodies.

TOAST AND WATER. Take a slice of fine and stale loaf-bread, cut very thin, (as thin as toast is ever cut) and let it be carefully toasted on both sides, until it be completely browned all over, but no wise blackened or burned in any way. Put this into a common deep stone or china jug, and pour over it, from the tea kettle, as much clean boiling water as you wish to make into drink. Much depends on the water being actually in a boiling state. Cover the jug with a saucer or plate, and let the drink stand until it be quite cold; it is then fit to be used; the fresher it is made the better, and of course the more agreeable. The above will be found a pleasant, light, and highly diuretic drink. It is peculiarly grateful to the stomach, and excellent for carrying off the effects of any excess in drinking. It is also a most excellent drink at meals, and may be used in the summer time, if more agreeable to the drinker.

TOASTED CHEESE. Mix some fine butter, made mustard, and salt, into a mass. Spread it on fresh made thin toasts, and grate some Gloucester cheese upon them.

TOMATOES. These are chiefly used in soups and sauces, and serve as little dishes at table at any part of a dinner. When they are to be baked, cut the tomatoes lengthways in the middle, with the part where there is a rind downwards. Strew upon each a seasoning of pepper, salt, and sweet herbs chopped small. Set them in the oven till they are soft, and serve them up, without any other sauce. The fruit of the purple egg plant is eaten, prepared in the same manner.

TOMATA SAUCE. For hot or cold meats put tomatas, when perfectly ripe, into an earthen jar. Set it in an oven when the bread is drawn, till they are quite soft; then separate the skins from the pulp, and mix this with capsicum vinegar, and a few cloves of pounded garlic, which must both be proportioned to the quantity of fruit. Add powdered ginger and salt to taste. Some white wine vinegar and cayenne may be used instead of capsicum vinegar. Keep the mixture in small wide-mouthed bottles, well corked, and in a cool dry place.

TONGUES. When a tongue is intended to be eaten cold, season it with common salt and saltpetre, brown sugar, a little bay salt, pepper, cloves, mace, and allspice, in fine powder, and let it lie a fortnight. Then take away the pickle, put the tongue into a small pan, and lay some butter on it. Cover it with brown crust, and bake it slowly till it becomes so tender that a straw would go through it. The thin part of tongues, when hung up to dry, grates like hung beef, and also makes a fine addition to the flavour of omlets.—To boil a tongue. If it is a dried tongue, soak it over night; the next day put it into cold water, and let it have a good deal of room; it will take at least four hours. If it is a green tongue out of the pickle, you need not soak it, but it will require near the same time. About an hour before you send it to table, take it out and blanch it, then put it into the pot again till you want it, by this means it will eat the tenderer.

TONGUE AND UDDER. Clean the tongue nicely, rub it with salt, a very little saltpetre, and a little coarse sugar, and let it lie for two or three days. When to be dressed, have a fresh tender udder with some fat to it, and boil that and the tongue gently till half done. Take them very clean out of the water, then tie the thick end of the one to the thin end of the other, and roast them with a few cloves stuck into the udder. Serve them up with gravy in the dish, and currant jelly in a tureen. A dried tongue to be boiled, requires to be previously soaked for ten or twelve hours. A tongue out of pickle is only to be washed, and boiled in the same way. It will take four hours to do it well, and for the first two hours it should only simmer. About an hour before it is done it should be taken up and peeled, and then put into the boiler again to finish it. Serve it up with turnips nicely mashed, and laid round it.

TOOTH ACH. The best possible preventive of this disorder is to keep the teeth clean, as directed for the Teeth and Gums. If the gums be inflamed, recourse should be had to bleeding by leeches, and blisters behind the ears. A few drops of laudanum in cotton, laid on the tooth, will sometimes afford relief. In some cases, vitriolic æther dropped on the cheek, and the hand held to the part till the liquid is evaporated, is found to answer the purpose. But it is much easier to prescribe the means of preventing the disorder, than to point out a specific remedy; and the nostrums generally given on this subject are either ineffectual or injurious.

TOURTE CRUST. To make a crust for French pies called tourtes, take a pound and a half of fine flour, a pound of butter, and three quarters of an ounce of salt. Put the flour upon a clean pie board, make a hole in the middle, and put in the salt, with the butter cut into small pieces. Pour in the water carefully, as it is of great importance that the crust be rather stiff; and for this purpose there should only be just water enough to make it hold together so as to roll it out smooth. Work up the butter and water well together with the hand, and mix it in the flour by degrees. When the flour is all mixed in, mould the paste till it is quite smooth and free from lumps, and let it lie two hours before it be used. This is a very nice crust for putting round the dish for baked puddings.

TOURTES OF FISH. Prepare the crust and put it into the dish, as for meat tourtes. Then take almost any kind of fish, cut them from the backbone, and lay them in slices upon the crust, with a little bunch of sweet herbs in the middle, some salt and pounded spice, according to the taste. Lay butter all over the top crust, and bake it an hour and a half. Cut the crust round after it is baked, take out the herbs, skim off the remainder of the fat, pour on a sauce of fish gravy, and serve it up. Mushrooms are very nice in the sauce, and so are capers, but the flavour of the sauce must be regulated by the taste. Truffles and morels may also be put in, as in the meat tourtes. Eels, pike, salmon, tench, whiting, are proper for the purpose. Nothing makes a nicer tourte in this way than large soles, taking off the flesh from the backbone, without the side fins. Lobsters also make an excellent tourte, and oysters are very nice mixed with other fish.

TOURTES OF MEAT. Prepare a crust of paste, roll it out, and line a dish with it not deeper than a common plate. Veal, chicken, pigeons, sweetbread, or game of any kind, may be prepared as follows. Cut in pieces whichever is preferred, just heat it in water, drain it, season it with pepper and salt, lay it upon the crust without piling it up high, and leave a border round the rim of the dish. Place some pieces of butter upon the meat to keep it moist, and add truffles, mushrooms, morels, artichoke bottoms, or forcemeat balls, at pleasure. Cover the whole with slices of fat bacon, and then lay a crust over it exactly corresponding with that underneath. Glaze over the upper crust with yolk of egg, and set the tourte into an oven. When it has been in a quarter of an hour, draw it to the mouth of the oven, and make a hole in the centre of the crust to let out the fumes. Let it stand nearly three hours longer in the oven, then take it out, cut the crust round with the rim, take it off, take out the bacon, and clear off any fat that may remain on the top. Have ready a rich ragout sauce to pour over it, then replace the crust, and serve it up. This dish is according to the French fashion.

TRANSPARENT MARMALADE. Cut the palest Seville oranges in quarters, take out the pulp, and put it in a bason, picking out the seeds and skins. Let the outsides soak in water with a little salt all night, then boil them in a good quantity of spring water till tender; drain, and cut them in very thin slices, and put them to the pulp. To every pound, add a pound and a half of double-refined sugar beaten fine; boil them together twenty minutes, but be careful not to break the slices. It must be stirred all the time very gently, and put into glasses when cold.

TRANSPARENT PAINTINGS. The paper must be fixed in a straining frame, in order to place it between the eye and the light, when required. After tracing the design, the colours must be laid on, in the usual method of stained drawings. When the tints are got in, place the picture against the window, on a pane of glass framed for the purpose, and begin to strengthen the shadows with Indian ink, or with colours, according as the effect requires; laying the colours sometimes on both sides of the paper, to give greater force and depth of colour. The last touches for giving final strength to shadows and forms, are to be done with ivory black or lamp black, prepared with gum water; as there is no pigment so opaque, and capable of giving strength and decision. When the drawing is finished, and every part has got its depth of colour and brilliancy, being perfectly dry, touch very carefully with spirits of turpentine, on both sides, those parts which are to be the brightest, such as the moon and fire; and those parts requiring less brightness, only on one side. Then lay on immediately with a pencil, a varnish made by dissolving one ounce of Canada balsam in an equal quantity of spirit of turpentine. Be cautious with the varnish, as it is apt to spread. When the varnish is dry, tinge the flame with red lead and gamboge, slightly touching the smoke next the flame. The moon must not be tinted with colour. Much depends on the choice of the subject, and none is so admirably adapted to this species of effect, as the gloomy Gothic ruin, whose antique towers and pointed turrets finely contrast their dark battlements with the pale yet brilliant moon. The effect of rays passing through the ruined windows, half choked with ivy; or of a fire among the clustering pillars and broken monuments of the choir, round which are figures of banditti, or others, whose haggard faces catch the reflecting light; afford a peculiarity of effect not to be equaled in any other species of painting. Internal views of cathedrals also, where windows of stained glass are introduced, have a beautiful effect. The great point to be attained is, a happy coincidence between the subject and the effect produced. The fine light should not be too near the moon, as its glare would tend to injure her pale silver light. Those parts which are not interesting, should be kept in an undistinguishing gloom; and where the principal light is, they should be marked with precision. Groups of figures should be well contrasted; those in shadow crossing those that are in light, by which means the opposition of light against shade is effected.

TRANSPARENT PUDDING. Beat up eight eggs, put them into a stewpan, with half a pound of sugar finely pounded, the same quantity of butter, and some grated nutmeg. Set it on the fire, and keep it stirring till it thickens. Then set it into a basin to cool, put a rich puff paste round the dish, pour in the pudding, and bake it in a moderate oven. It will cut light and clear. Candied orange and citron may be added if approved.

TRANSPLANTING OF FLOWERS. Annuals and perennials, sown in March or April, may be transplanted about the end of May. A showery season is preferable, or they must frequently be watered till they have taken root. In the summer time the evening is the proper season, and care should be taken not to break the fibres in digging up the root. Chinasters, columbines, marigolds, pinks, stocks, hollyhocks, mallows, sweetwilliams, wallflowers, and various others, may be sown and transplanted in this manner.

TRAPS. Garden traps, such as are contrived for the purpose of destroying mice and other vermin; which are often conveyed into such places with the straw, litter, and other matters that are made use of in them; and which are extremely hurtful and troublesome in the spring season, in destroying peas and beans, as well as lettuces, melons, and cucumbers in frames. Traps for this purpose are contrived in a great many ways; but as field vermin are very shy, and will rarely enter traps which are close, the following simple cheap form has been advised, though it has nothing of novelty in it. These traps may be made by stringing garden beans on a piece of fine pack-thread, in the manner of beads, and then driving two small stake-like pieces of wood into the ground at the breadth of a brick from each other, and setting up a brick, flat stone, or board with a weight on it, inclining to an angle of about forty-five degrees; tying the string, with the beans on it, round the brick or other substances and stakes, to support them in their inclining position, being careful to place all the beans on the under sides of the bricks or other matters. The mice in eating the beans, in such cases, will also destroy the pack-thread, and by such means disengage the brick or other weighty body, which by falling on them readily destroys them. Mice are always best got rid of by some sort of simple open traps of this nature.

TREACLE BEER. Pour two quarts of boiling water on a pound of treacle, and stir them together. Add six quarts of cold water, and a tea-cupful of yeast. Tun it into a cask, cover it close down, and it will be fit to drink in two or three days. If made in large quantities, or intended to keep, put in a handful of malt and hops, and when the fermentation is over, stop it up close.

TREACLE POSSET. Add two table-spoonfuls of treacle to a pint of milk, and when ready to boil, stir it briskly over the fire till it curdles. Strain it off after standing covered a few minutes. This whey promotes perspiration, is suitable for a cold, and children will take it very freely.

TREATMENT OF CHILDREN. It ought to be an invariable rule with all who have the care of children, to give them food only when it is needful. Instead of observing this simple and obvious rule, it is too common, throughout every period of childhood, to pervert the use of food by giving it when it is not wanted, and consequently when it does mischief, not only in a physical but in a moral point of view. To give food as an indulgence, or in a way of reward, or to withhold it as a matter of punishment, are alike injurious. A proper quantity of food is necessary in all cases, to sustain their health and growth; and their faults ought to be corrected by more rational means. The idea of making them suffer in their health and growth on account of their behaviour, is sufficient to fill every considerate mind with horror. It is the project only of extreme weakness, to attempt to correct the disposition by creating bodily sufferings, which are so prone to hurt the temper, even at an age when reason has gained a more powerful ascendancy. Eatables usually given to children by well-meaning but injudicious persons, in order to pacify or conciliate, are still worse than the privations inflicted by way of punishment. Sugar plums, sugar candy, barley sugar, sweetmeats, and most kinds of cakes, are unwholesome, and cloying to the appetite. Till children begin to run about, the uniformity of their lives makes it probable that the quantity of food they require in the day is nearly the same, and that it may be given to them stately at the same time. By establishing a judicious regularity with regard to both, much benefit will accrue to their health and comfort. The same rule should be applied to infants at the breast, as well as after they are weaned. By allowing proper intervals between the times of giving children suck, the breast of the mother becomes duly replenished with milk, and the stomach of the infant properly emptied to receive a fresh supply. The supposition that an infant wants food every time it cries, is highly fanciful; and it is perfectly ridiculous to see the poor squalling thing thrown on its back, and nearly suffocated with food to prevent its crying, when it is more likely that the previous uneasiness arises from an overloaded stomach. Even the mother's milk, the lightest of all food, will disagree with the child, if the administration of it is improperly repeated. A very injurious practice is sometimes adopted, in suckling a child beyond the proper period, which ought by all means to be discountenanced, as evidently unnatural, and tending to produce weakness both in body and mind. Suckling should not be continued after the cutting of the first teeth, when the clearest indication is given, that the food which was adapted to the earliest stage of infancy ceases to be proper. Attention should also be paid to the quantity as well as to quality of the food given, for though a child will sleep with an overloaded stomach, it will not be the refreshing sleep of health. When the stomach is filled beyond the proper medium, it induces a similar kind of heaviness to that arising from opiates and intoxicating liquors; and instead of awakening refreshed and lively, the child will be heavy and fretful. By the time that children begin to run about, the increase of their exercise will require an increase of nourishment: but those who overload them with food at any time, in hopes of strengthening them, are very much deceived. No prejudice is equally fatal to such numbers of children. Whatever unnecessary food a child receives, weakens instead of strengthening it: for when the stomach is overfilled, its power of digestion is impaired, and food undigested is so far from yielding nourishment, that it only serves to debilitate the whole system, and to occasion a variety of diseases. Amongst these are obstructions, distention of the body, rickets, scrophula, slow fevers, consumptions, and convulsion fits. Another pernicious custom prevails with regard to the diet of children, when they begin to take other nourishment besides their mother's milk, and that is by giving them such as their stomachs are unable to digest, and indulging them also in a mixture of such things at their meals as are hurtful to every body, and more especially to children, considering the feeble and delicate state of their organs. This injudicious indulgence is sometimes defended on the plea of its being necessary to accustom them to all kinds of food; but this idea is highly erroneous. Their stomachs must have time to acquire strength sufficient to enable them to digest varieties of food; and the filling them with indigestible things is not the way to give them strength. Children can only acquire strength gradually with their proper growth, which will always be impeded if the stomach is disordered. Food for infants should be very simple, and easy of digestion. When they require something more solid than spoonmeats alone, they should have bread with them. Plain puddings, mild vegetables, and wholesome ripe fruits, eaten with bread, are also good for them. Animal food is better deferred till their increased capacity for exercise will permit it with greater safety, and then care must be taken that the exercise be proportioned to this kind of food. The first use of it should be gradual, not exceeding two or three times in a week. An exception should be made to these rules in the instances of scrophulous and rickety children, as much bread is always hurtful in these cases, and fruits are particularly pernicious. Plain animal food is found to be the most suitable to their state. The utmost care should be taken under all circumstances to procure genuine unadulterated bread for children, as the great support of life. If the perverted habits of the present generation give them an indifference as to what bread they eat, or a vitiated taste for adulterated bread, they still owe it to their children as a sacred duty, not to undermine their constitution by this injurious composition. The poor, and many also of the middling ranks of society are unhappily compelled to this species of infanticide, as it may almost be called, by being driven into large towns to gain a subsistence, and thus, from the difficulty of doing otherwise, being obliged to take their bread of bakers, instead of making wholesome bread at home, as in former times, in more favourable situations. While these are to be pitied, what shall be said of those whose fortunes place them above this painful necessity. Let them at at least rear their children on wholesome food, and with unsophisticated habits, as the most unequivocal testimony of parental affection performing its duty towards its offspring. It is proper also to observe, that children ought not to be hurried in their eating, as it is of great importance that they should acquire a habit of chewing their food well. They will derive from it the various advantages of being less likely to eat their food hot, of thus preparing what they eat properly for the stomach, instead of imposing upon it what is the real office of the teeth; and also that of checking them from eating too much. When food is not properly masticated, the stomach is longer before it feels satisfied; which is perhaps the most frequent, and certainly the most excusable cause of eating more than is fairly sufficient. Thoughtless people will often, for their own amusement, give children morsels of high dishes, and sips of spirituous or fermented liquors, to see whether they will relish them, or make faces at them. But trifling as this may seem, it would be better that it were never practised, for the sake of preserving the natural purity of their tastes as long as possible.

TREATMENT OF THE SICK. Though an unskilful dabbling in cases of illness, which require the attention of the most medical practitioners, is both dangerous and presumptuous; yet it is quite necessary that those who have the care of a family should be able to afford some relief in case of need, as well as those whose duty it is more immediately to attend upon the sick. Uneasy symptoms are experienced at times by all persons, not amounting to a decided state of disease, which if neglected may nevertheless issue in some serious disorder that might have been prevented, not only without risk, but even with greater advantage to the individual than by an application to a positive course of medicine. Attention to the state of the bowels, and the relief that may frequently be afforded by a change of diet, come therefore very properly within the sphere of domestic management, in connection with a few simple medicines in common use. The sensations of lassitude or weariness, stiffness or numbness, less activity than usual, less appetite, a load or heaviness at the stomach, some uneasiness in the head, a more profound degree of sleep, yet less composed and refreshing than usual; less gaiety and liveliness, a slight oppression of the breast, a less regular pulse, a propensity to be cold, or to perspire, or sometimes a suppression of a former disposition to perspire, are any of them symptomatic of a diseased state, though not to any very serious or alarming degree. Yet under such circumstances persons are generally restless, and scarcely know what to do with themselves; and often for the sake of change, or on the supposition that their sensations proceed from lowness, they unhappily adopt the certain means of making them terminate in dangerous if not fatal diseases. They increase their usual quantity of animal food, leave off vegetables and fruit, drink freely of wine or other strong liquors, under an idea of strengthening the stomach, and expelling wind; all of which strengthen nothing but the disposition to disease, and expel only the degree of health yet remaining. The consequence of this mistaken management is, that all the evacuations are restrained, the humours causing and nourishing the disease are not at all attempered and diluted, nor rendered proper for evacuation. On the contrary they become sharper, and more difficult to be discharged. By judicious management it is practicable, if not entirely to prevent a variety of disorders, yet at least to abate their severity, and so to avert the ultimate danger. As soon as any of the symptoms begin to appear, the proper way is to avoid all violent or laborious exercise, and to indulge in such only as is gentle and easy. To take very little or no solid food, and particularly to abstain from meat, or flesh broth, eggs, and wine, or other strong liquors. To drink plentifully of weak diluting liquor, by small glasses at a time, at intervals of about half an hour. If these diluents are not found to answer the purpose of keeping the bowels open, stronger cathartics must be taken, or injections for the bowels, called lavements. By pursuing these precautions, the early symptoms of disease will often be removed, without coming to any serious issue: and even where this is not the case, the disorder will be so lessened as to obviate any kind of danger from it. When confirmed diseases occur, the only safe course is to resort to the most skilful medical assistance that can be obtained. Good advice and few medicines will much sooner effect a cure, than all the drugs of the apothecary's shop unskilfully administered. But the success of the best advice may be defeated, if the patient and his attendants will not concur to render it effectual. If the patient is to indulge longings for improper diet, and his friends are to gratify them, the advantage of the best advice may be defeated by one such imprudent measure. Patients labouring under accidents which require surgical assistance, must be required strictly to attend to the same directions. General regulations are all that a physician or surgeon can make respecting diet, many other circumstances will therefore require the consideration of those who attend upon the sick, and it is of consequence that they be well prepared to undertake their charge, for many fatal mistakes have arisen from ignorance and prejudice in these cases. A few rules that may be referred to in the absence of a medical adviser, are all that are necessary in the present instance, more especially when the patient is so far recovered as to be released from medicines, and put under a proper regimen, with the use of a gentle exercise, and such other regulations as a convalescent state requires.—When for example, persons are labouring under acute disorders, or accidents, they are frequently known to suffer from the injudiciousness of those about them, in covering them up in bed with a load of clothes that heat and debilitate them exceedingly, or in keeping them in bed when the occasion does not require it, without even suffering them to get up and have it new made, and by never allowing a breath of fresh air to be admitted into the room. The keeping patients quiet is undoubtedly of essential importance; they should not be talked to, nor should more persons be admitted into the room than are absolutely necessary. Every thing that might prove offensive should immediately be removed. Sprinkling the room sometimes with vinegar, will contribute to keep it in a better state. The windows should be opened occasionally for a longer or shorter time, according to the weather and season of the year, without suffering the air to come immediately upon the patient. Waving the chamber door backward and forward for a few minutes, two or three times in a day, ventilates the room, without exposing the sick person to chilness. Occasionally burning pastils in the room, or a roll of paper, is also useful. The bed linen, and that of the patient, should be changed every day, or in two or three days, as circumstances may require. A strict forbearance from giving sick persons any nourishment beyond what is prescribed by their medical attendant, should invariably be observed. Some persons think they do well in this respect to cheat the doctor, while in fact they cheat the patient out of the benefit of his advice, and endanger his life under a pretence of facilitating his recovery. In all cases it is important to wait with patience the slow progress of recovery, rather than by injudicious means to attempt to hasten it; otherwise the desired event will only be retarded. What has long been undermining the stamina of health, which is commonly the case with diseases, or what has violently shocked it by accident, can only be removed by slow degrees. Medicines will not operate like a charm; and even when they are most efficacious, time is required to recover from the languid state to which persons are always reduced, both by accident and by disease. When the period is arrived at which sick persons may be said to be out of danger, a great deal of patience and care will still be necessary to prevent a relapse. Much of this will depend on the convalescent party being content for some time with only a moderate portion of food, for we are not nourished in proportion to what we swallow, but to what we are well able to digest. Persons on their recovery, who eat moderately, digest their food, and grow strong from it. Those in a weak state, who eat much, do not digest it; instead therefore of being nourished and strengthened by it, they insensibly wither away. The principal rules to be observed in this case are, that persons in sickness, or those who are slowly recovering, should take very little nourishment at a time, and take it often. Let them have only one sort of food at each meal, and not change their food too often; and be careful that they chew their food well, to make it easy of digestion. Let them diminish their quantity of drink. The best drink for them in general is water, with a third or fourth part of white wine. Too great a quantity of liquids at such a time prevents the stomach from recovering its tone and strength, impairs digestion, promotes debility, increases the tendency to a swelling of the legs; sometimes it even occasions a slow fever, and throws back the patient into a languid state. Persons recovering from sickness should take as much exercise in the open air as they are able to bear, either on foot, in a carriage, or on horseback: the latter is by far the best. The airing should be taken in the middle of the day, when the weather is temperate, or before the principal meal. Exercise taken before a meal strengthens the organs of digestion, and therefore tends to health; but when taken after a meal, it is injurious. As persons in this state are seldom quite so well towards night, they should take very little food in the evening, in order that their sleep may be less disturbed and more refreshing. It would be better not to remain in bed above seven or eight hours; and if they feel fatigued by sitting up, let them lie down for half an hour to rest. The swelling of the legs and ancles, which happens to most persons in a state of weakness and debility, is attended with no danger, and will generally disappear of itself, if they live soberly and regularly, and take moderate exercise. The most solicitous attention must be paid to the state of the bowels; and if they are not regular, they must be kept open every day by artificial means, or it will produce heat and restlessness, and pains in the head. Care should be taken not to return to hard labour too soon after recovering from illness; some persons have never recovered their usual strength for want of this precaution.—Common colds, though lightly regarded, are often of serious consequence. A cold is an inflammatory disease, though in no greater degree than to affect the lungs or throat, or the thin membrane which lines the nostrils, and the inside of certain cavities in the bones of the cheeks and forehead. These cavities communicate with the nose in such a manner, that when one part of this membrane is affected with inflammation, it is easily communicated to the rest. When the disorder is of this slight kind, it may easily be cured without medicine, by only abstaining from meat, eggs, broth, and wine; from all food that is sharp, fat, and heavy. Little or no supper should be eaten, but the person should drink freely of an infusion of barley, or of elder flowers, with the addition of a third or fourth part of milk. Bathing the feet in warm water before going to bed, will dispose the patient to sleep. In colds of the head, the steam of warm water alone, or of water in which elder flowers or some mild aromatic herbs have been boiled, will generally afford speedy relief. These also are serviceable in colds which affect the breast. Hot and close rooms are very hurtful in colds, as they tend to impede respiration; and sitting much over the fire increases the disorder. Spermaceti is often taken in colds and coughs, which must from its greasy nature impair the digestive faculty, and cannot operate against the cause of a cold; though the cure of it, which is effected in due time by the economy of nature, is often ascribed to such medicines as may rather have retarded it. Whenever a cold does not yield to the simple treatment already described, good advice should be procured, as a neglected cold is often the origin of very serious disorders.—A few observations on the nature of the diet and drink proper for sickly persons, will be necessary at the close of this article, for the information of those who occasionally undertake the care of the afflicted. As the digestion of sick persons is weak, and very similar to that of children, the diet suited to the latter is generally proper for the former, excepting in the two great classes of diseases called putrid and intermittent fevers. In case of putrid fever no other food should be allowed, during the first weeks of recovery, than the mildest vegetable substances. When recovering from agues and intermittent fevers, animal jellies, and plain animal food, with as little vegetable as possible, is the proper diet. Meat and meat broth, generally speaking, are not so well adapted for the re-establishment of health and strength, as more simple diets. Flesh being the food most used by old and young at all other times, is consequently that from which their distempers chiefly proceed, or at least it nourishes those disorders which other causes may have contributed to introduce. It is of a gross, phlegmatic nature and oily quality, and therefore harder of digestion than many other sorts of food, tending to generate gross humours and thick blood, which are very unfavourable to the recovery of health. The yolk of an egg lightly boiled or beaten up raw with a little wine may be taken, when animal food is not forbidden, and the party cannot chew or swallow more solid food. The spoonmeats and drinks directed for children, and simple puddings made as for them, may all be used for invalids, subject only to the restrictions imposed by their medical attendant. Puddings and panadoes made of bread are better for weak stomachs than those made of flour.—Diet drinks may be made of an infusion of herbs, grains, or seeds. For this purpose the herbs should be gathered in their proper season, then dried in the shade, and put into close paper bags. When wanted for use, take out the proper quantity, put it into a linen bag, suspend it in the beer or ale, while it is fermenting, from two to six or eight hours, and then take it out. Wormwood ought not to be infused so long; three or four hours will be sufficient, or it will become nauseous, and soon turn to putrefaction. The same is to be understood in infusing any sort of well-prepared herbs, and great care is required in all preparations of this kind that the pure properties are neither evaporated, nor overpowered by the bad ones. Beer, ale, or any other liquor in which herbs are infused, must be unadulterated, or the benefit of these infusions will be destroyed by its pernicious qualities. Nothing is more prejudicial to health than adulterated liquors, or liquors that are debased by any corrupting vegetable substance. Those things which in their purest state are of a doubtful character, and never to be trusted without caution, are by this means converted into decided poisons.—Herb Tea of any kind should always be made with a moderate proportion of the herb. When the tea is of a proper strength, the herb should be taken out, or it will become nauseous by long infusion. These kinds of tea are best used quite fresh.—Herb Porridge may be made of elder buds, nettle tops, clivers, and water cresses. Mix up a proper quantity of oatmeal and water, and set it on the fire. When just ready to boil, put in the herbs, cut or uncut; and when ready again to boil, lade it to and fro to prevent its boiling. Continue this operation six or eight minutes, then take it off the fire, and let it stand awhile. It may either be eaten with the herbs, or strained, and should not be eaten warmer than new milk. A little butter, salt, and bread, may be added. Another way is, to set some oatmeal and water on a quick fire; and when it is scalding hot, put in a good quantity of spinage, corn salad, tops of pennyroyal, and mint cut small. Let it stand on the fire till ready to boil, then pour it up and down six or seven minutes, and let it stand off the fire that the oatmeal may sink to the bottom. Strain it, and add butter, salt, and bread. When it is about milk-warm it will be fit to eat. This is an excellent porridge, pleasant to the palate and stomach, cleansing the passages by opening obstructions. It also breeds good blood, thus enlivens the spirits, and makes the whole body active and easy.—A Cooling Drink may be made of two ounces of whole barley, washed and cleansed in hot water, and afterwards boiled in five pints of water till the barley opens. Add a quarter of an ounce of cream of tartar, and strain off the liquor. Or bruise three ounces of the freshest sweet almonds, and an ounce of gourd melon seeds in a marble mortar, adding a pint of water, a little at a time, and then strain it through a piece of linen. Bruise the remainder of the almonds and seeds again, with another pint of water added as before; then strain it, and repeat this process a third time. After this, pour all the liquor upon the bruised mass, stir it well, and finally strain it off. Half an ounce of sugar may safely be bruised with the almonds and seeds at first; or if it be thought too heating, a little orange-flower water may be used instead.—Currant Drink. Put a pound of the best red currants, fully ripe and clean picked, into a stone bottle. Mix three spoonfuls of good new yeast with six pints of hot water, and pour it upon the currants. Stop the bottle close till the liquor ferments, then give it as much vent as is necessary, keep it warm, and let it ferment for about three days. Taste it in the mean time to try whether it is become pleasant; and as soon as it is so, run it through a strainer, and bottle it off. It will be ready to drink in five or six days.—Boniclapper is another article suited to the state of sickly and weakly persons. Boniclapper is milk which has stood till it has acquired a pleasant sourish taste, and a thick slippery substance. In very hot weather this will be in about twenty-four hours from the time of its being milked, but longer in proportion as the weather is colder. If put into vessels which have been used for milk to be soured in, it will change the sooner. New milk must always be used for this purpose. Boniclapper is an excellent food at all times, particularly for those who are troubled with any kind of stoppages; it powerfully opens the breast and passages, is itself easy of digestion, and helps to digest all hard or sweeter foods. It also cools and cleanses the whole body, renders it brisk and lively, and is very efficacious in quenching thirst. No other sort of milkmeat or spoonmeat is so proper and beneficial for consumptive persons, or such as labour under great weakness and debility. It should be eaten with bread only, and it will be light and easy on the stomach, even when new milk is found to disagree. If this soured milk should become unpleasant at first, a little custom and use will not only render it familiar, but agreeable to the stomach and palate; and those who have neither wisdom nor patience to submit to a transient inconvenience, will never have an opportunity of knowing the intrinsic value of any thing. To these may be added a variety of other articles adapted to a state of sickness and disease, which will be found under their respective heads; such as Beef Tea, Flummery, Jellies of various kinds, Lemon Whey, Vinegar Whey, Cream of Tartar Whey, Mustard Whey, Treacle Posset, Buttermilk, Onion Porridge, Water Gruel, and Wormwood Ale.

TREES. Several different methods have been proposed of preventing the bark being eaten off by hares and rabbits in the winter season; such as twisting straw-ropes round the trees; driving in small flat stakes all about them; and the use of strong-scented oils. But better and neater modes have lately been suggested; as with hog's lard, and as much whale-oil as will work it up into a thin paste or paint, with which the stems of the trees are to be gently rubbed upwards, at the time of the fall of the leaf. It may be done once in two years, and will, it is said, effectually prevent such animals from touching them. Another and still neater method, is to take three pints of melted tallow to one pint of tar, mixing them well together over a gentle fire. Then, in the month of November, to take a small brush and go over the rind or bark of the trees with the composition in a milk-warm state, as thin as it can be laid on with the brush. It is found that such a coating does not hinder the juices or sap from expanding in the smallest degree; and the efficacy of the plan is proved, in preventing the attacks of the animals, by applying the liquid composition to one tree and missing another, when it was found that the former was left, while the latter was attacked. Its efficacy has been shewn by the experience of five years. The trees that were gone over the first two years have not been touched since; and none of them have been injured by the hares.—The Mossing of trees is their becoming much affected and covered with the moss-plant or mossy substance. It is found to prevail in fruit-grounds of the apple kind, and in other situations, when they are in low, close, confined places, where the damp or moisture of the trees is not readily removed. It is thought to be an indication of weakness in the growth, or of a diseased state of the trees, and to require nice attention in preventing or eradicating it. The modes of removing it have usually been those of scraping, rubbing, and washing, but they are obviously calculated for trees only on a small scale. How far the use of powdery matters, such as lime, chalk, and others, which are capable of readily absorbing and taking up the wetness that may hang about the branches, and other parts of the trees, by being well dusted over them, may be beneficial, is not known, but they would seem to promise success by the taking away the nourishment and support of the moss, when employed at proper seasons. And they are known to answer in destroying moss in some other cases, when laid about the stems of the plants, as in thorn-hedges, &c. The mossing in all sorts of trees is injurious to their growth by depriving them of a portion of their nourishment, but more particularly hurtful to those of the fruit-tree kind, as preventing them from bearing full good crops of fruit by rendering them in a weak and unhealthy state.——The following are substances destructive of insects infesting fruit shrubs and trees in gardening, or of preventing their injurious ravages and effects on trees. Many different kinds of substances have been recommended for the purpose, at different times; but nothing perhaps has yet been found fully effectual in this intention, in all cases. The substances and modes directed below have lately been advised as useful in this way. As preventives against gooseberry caterpillars, which so greatly infest and injure shrubs of that kind, the substances mentioned below have been found very simple and efficacious. In the autumnal season, let a quantity of cow-urine be provided, and let a little be poured around the stem of each bush or shrub, just as much as merely suffices to moisten the ground about them. This simple expedient is stated to have succeeded in an admirable manner, and that its preventive virtues have appeared to extend to two successive seasons or years. The bushes which were treated in this manner remained free from caterpillars, while those which were neglected, or intentionally passed by, in the same compartment, were wholly destroyed by the depredations of the insects. Another mode of prevention is proposed, which, it is said, is equally simple and effectual; but the good effects of which only extend to the season immediately succeeding to that of the application. This is, in situations near the sea, to collect as much drift or sea-weed from the beach, when occasion serves, as will be sufficient to cover the whole of the gooseberry compartment to the depth of four or five inches. It should be laid on in the autumn, and the whole covering remain untouched during the winter and early spring months; but as the fruiting season advances, be dug in. This method, it is said, has answered the most sanguine expectations; no caterpillars ever infesting the compartments which are treated in this manner. Another method, which is said to have been found successful, in preventing or destroying caterpillars on the above sort of fruit shrubs, is this: as the black currant and elder bushes, growing quite close to those of the gooseberry kind, were not attacked by this sort of vermin, it was conceived that an infusion of their leaves might be serviceable, especially when prepared with a little quick-lime, in the manner directed below. Six pounds each of the two first sorts of leaves are to be boiled in twelve gallons of soft water; then fourteen pounds of hot lime are to be put into twelve gallons of water, and, after being well incorporated with it, they are both to be mixed well together. With this mixture the infested gooseberry bushes by fruit trees are to be well washed or the hand garden-engine; after which a little hot lime is to be taken and laid about the root of each bush or tree so washed, which completes the work. Thus the caterpillars will be completely destroyed, without hurting the foliage of the bushes or trees in any way. A dull day is to be preferred for performing the work of washing, &c. As soon as all the foliage is dropped off from the bushes or trees, they are to be again washed over with the hand-engine, in order to clean them of all decayed leaves, and other matters; for which purpose any sort of water will answer. The surface of the earth, all about the roots of the bushes and trees, is then to be well stirred, and a little hot lime again laid about them, to destroy the ova or eggs of the insects. This mode of management has never failed of success, in the course of six years' practice. It is noticed, that the above quantity of prepared liquid will be sufficient for about two acres of ground in this sort of plantation, and cost but little in providing. The use of about a gallon of a mixture of equal proportions of lime-water, chamber-ley, and soap-suds, with as much soot as will give it the colour and consistence of dunghill drainings, to each bush in the rows, applied by means of the rose of a watering-pot, immediately as the ground between them is dug over, and left as rough as possible, the whole being gone over in this way without treading or poaching the land, has also been found highly successful by others. The whole is then left in the above state until the winter frosts are fairly past, when the ground between the rows and bushes are levelled, and raked over in an even manner. By this means of practice, the bushes have been constantly kept healthy, fruitful, and free from the annoyance of insects. The bushes are to be first pruned, and dung used where necessary. A solution of soft soap, mixed with an infusion of tobacco, has likewise been applied with great use in destroying caterpillars, by squirting it by the hand-syringe upon the bushes, while a little warm, twice in the day. But some think that the only safety is in picking them off the bushes, as they first appear, together with the lower leaves which are eaten into holes: also, the paring, digging over, and clearing the foul ground between the bushes, and treading and forcing such foul surface parts into the bottoms of the trenches. Watering cherry-trees with water prepared from quick-lime new burnt, and common soda used in washing, in the proportion of a peck of the former and half a pound of the latter to a hogshead of water, has been found successful in destroying the green fly and the black vermin which infest such trees. The water should stand upon the lime for twenty-four hours, and be then drawn off by a cock placed in the cask, ten or twelve inches from the bottom, when the soda is to be put to it, being careful not to exceed the above proportion, as, from its acridity, it would otherwise be liable to destroy the foliage. Two or three times watering with this liquor, by means of a garden engine, will destroy and remove the vermin. The application of clay-paint, too, has been found of great utility in destroying the different insects, such as the coccus, thrips, and fly, which infest peach, nectarine, and other fine fruit trees, on walls, and in hot-houses. This paint is prepared by taking a quantity of the most tenacious brown clay, and diffusing it in as much soft water as will bring it to the consistence of a thick cream or paint, passing it through a fine sieve or hair-searce, so as that it may be rendered perfectly smooth, unctuous, and free from gritty particles. As soon as the trees are pruned and nailed in, they are all to be carefully gone over with a painter's brush dipped in the above paint, especially the stems and large branches, as well as the young shoots, which leaves a coat or layer, that, when it becomes dry, forms a hard crust over the whole tree, which, by closely enveloping the insects, completely destroys them, without doing any injury to either the bark or buds. And by covering the trees with mats or canvas in wet seasons, it may be preserved on them as long as necessary. Where one dressing is not effectual, it may be repeated; and the second coating will mostly be sufficient. Where peach and nectarine trees are managed with this paint, they are very rarely either hide-bound or attacked by insects. This sort of paint is also useful in removing the mildew, with which these kinds of trees are often affected; as well as, with the use of the dew-syringe, in promoting the equal breaking of the eyes of vines, trained on the rafters of pine stoves. Watering the peach tree borders with the urine of cattle, in the beginning of winter, and again in the early spring, has likewise been thought beneficial in destroying the insects which produce the above disease. Careful and proper cleaning and washing these trees, walls, and other places in contact with them, has, too, been found of great utility in preventing insects from accumulating on them.

TRIFLE. To make an excellent trifle, lay macaroons and ratifia drops over the bottom of a dish, and pour in as much raisin wine as they will imbibe. Then pour on them a cold rich custard, made with plenty of eggs, and some rice flour. It must stand two or three inches thick: on that put a layer of raspberry jam, and cover the whole with a very high whip made the day before, of rich cream, the whites of two well-beaten eggs, sugar, lemon peel, and raisin wine, well beat with a whisk, kept only to whip syllabubs and creams. If made the day before it is used, the trifle has quite a different taste, and is solid and far better.

TRIPE. After being well washed and cleaned, tripe should be stewed with milk and onion till quite tender. Serve it in a tureen, with melted butter for sauce. Or fry it in small pieces, dipped in batter. Or cut the thin part into bits, and stew them in gravy. Thicken the stew with butter and flour, and add a little ketchup. Tripe may also be fricasseed with white sauce.

TROUGHS. Water troughs of various kinds, which require to be rendered impervious to the wet, may be lined with a strong cement of gypsum and quicklime, mixed up with water. Four fifths of pulverised coal or charcoal, and one fifth of quicklime, well mixed together, and infused in boiling pitch or tar, will also form a useful cement for this purpose. It requires to be of the consistence of thin mortar, and applied hot with a trowel.

TROUT. Open them along the belly, wash them clean, dry them in a cloth, and season them with pepper and salt. Set the gridiron over the fire, and when it is hot rub the bars with a piece of fresh suet. Lay on the fish, and broil them gently over a very clear fire, at such a distance as not to burn them. When they are done on one side, turn them carefully on the other, and serve them up the moment they are ready. This is one of the best methods of dressing this delicate fish; but they are sometimes broiled whole, in order to preserve the juices of the fish, when they are fresh caught. Another way is, after they are washed clean and well dried in a napkin, to bind them about with packthread, and sprinkle them with melted butter and salt; then to broil them over a gentle fire, and keep them turning. Make a sauce of butter rolled in flour, with an anchovy, some pepper, nutmeg, and capers. Add a very little vinegar and water, and shake it together over a moderate fire, till it is of a proper thickness. Put the trout into a dish, and pour this sauce over them. Trout of a middle size are best for broiling. The gurnet or piper is very nice broiled in the same manner, and served with the same kind of sauce. Mullets also admit of the same treatment. Trout are very commonly stewed, as well as broiled; and in this case they should be put into a stewpan with equal quantities of Champaigne, Rhenish, or Sherry wine. Season the stew with pepper and salt, an onion, a few cloves, and a small bunch of parsley and thyme. Put into it a crust of French bread, and set it on a quick fire. When the fish is done, take out the bread, bruise it, and then thicken the sauce. Add a little flour and butter, and let it boil up. Lay the trout on a dish, and pour the thickened sauce over it. Serve it with sliced lemon, and fried bread. This is called Trout á la Genevoise. A plainer way is to dry the fish, after it has been washed and cleaned, and lay it on a board before the fire, dusted with flour. Then fry it of a fine colour with fresh dripping; serve it with crimp parsley and plain butter.

TROUT PIE. Scale and wash the fish, lard them with pieces of silver eel, rolled up in spice and sweet herbs, with bay leaves finely powdered. Slice the bottoms of artichokes, lay them on or between the fish, with mushrooms, oysters, capers, and sliced lemon or Seville orange. Use a dish or raised crust, close the pie, and bake it gently.—Another way. Clean and scale your trouts, and cut off the heads and fins; boil an eel for forcemeat; when you have cut off the meat of the eel, put the bones and the heads of the trout into the water it was boiled in, with an onion, mace, whole pepper, a little salt, and a faggot of sweet herbs; let it boil down till there is but enough for the pie. Chop the meat of the eel very fine, add grated bread, an anchovy chopped small, sweet herbs, and a gill of oysters blanched and bearded, the yolks of two hard eggs chopped very fine, and as much melted butter as will make it into a stiff forcemeat; season the trout with mace, pepper and salt; fill the belly with the forcemeat, and make the remainder into balls; sheet your dish with a good paste, lay some butter on that, then the trout and forcemeat; strain off the fish broth, and scum it very clean, and add a little white wine, and a piece of butter rolled in flour; when it is all melted, pour it into the pie, and lid it over; bake it in a gentle oven, and let it be thoroughly done.

TRUFFLES. The largest are the most esteemed; those which are brought from Perigord are the best. They are usually eaten dressed in wine, and broth seasoned with salt, pepper, a bunch of sweet herbs, some roots and onions. Before being dressed they must be soaked in warm water, and well rubbed with a brush, that no earth may adhere to them. When dressed, serve them in a plate as an entremet. The truffle is also very excellent in all sorts of ragouts, either chopped or out into slices, after they are peeled. It is one of the best seasonings that can be used in a kitchen. Truffles are also used dried, but their flavour is then much diminished.

TRUFFLES RAGOUT. Peel the truffles, cut them in slices, wash and drain them well. Put them into a saucepan with a little gravy, and stew them gently over a slow fire. When they are almost done enough, thicken them with a little butter and flour. Stewed in a little water, and thickened with cream and yolk of egg, they make a nice white ragout. Truffles, mushrooms, and morels are all of them very indigestible.

TUNBRIDGE CAKES. Rub six ounces of butter quite fine into a pound of flour; then mix six ounces of sugar, beat and strain two eggs, and make the whole into a paste. Roll it very thin, and cut it with the top of a glass. Prick the cakes with a fork, and cover them with carraways; or wash them with the white of an egg, and dust a little white sugar over.

TURBOT. This excellent fish is in season the greatest part of the summer. When fresh and good, it is at once firm and tender, and abounds with rich gelatinous nutriment. Being drawn and washed clean, it may be lightly rubbed with salt, and put in a cold place, and it will keep two or three days. An hour or two before dressing it, let it soak in spring water with some salt in it. To prevent the fish from swelling and cracking on the breast, score the skin across the thickest part of the back. Put a large handful of salt into a fish kettle with cold water, lay the turbot on a fish strainer and put it in. When it is beginning to boil, skim it well; then set the kettle on the side of the fire to boil as gently as possible for about fifteen or twenty minutes; if it boil fast, the fish will break to pieces. Rub a little of the inside coral spawn of the lobster through a hair sieve, without butter; and when the turbot is dished, sprinkle the spawn over it. Garnish the dish with sprigs of curled parsley, sliced lemon, and finely scraped horseradish. Send up plenty of lobster sauce. The thickest part of the fish is generally preferred. The spine bone should be cut across to make it easier for carving.

TURBOT PIE. Take a middling turbot, clean it very well, cut off the head, tail, and fins. Make a forcemeat thus; take a large eel, boil it tender, then take off the flesh; put the bones of the turbot and eel into the water the eel was boiled in, with a faggot of herbs, whole pepper, an onion, and an anchovy; let this boil till it becomes a strong broth. In the mean time, cut the eel very fine; add the same quantity of grated bread, a little lemon-peel, an anchovy, parsley, and the yolks of two or three hard eggs, and half a pint of oysters blanched and bearded; chop all these as fine as possible; mix all together with a quarter of a pound of melted butter; and with this forcemeat lay a rim in the inside of the dish; put in the turbot, and fill up the vacancies with forcemeat; strain off the broth, scum it very clean, and add a lump of butter rolled in flour, and a glass of white wine; pour this over the fish. Make a good puff paste, cover the pie with it, and let it be thoroughly baked. When it comes from the oven, warm the remainder of the liquor; pour it in, and send it to table.

TURKEYS. When young they are very tender, and require great attention. As soon as hatched, put three peppercorns down their throat. They must be carefully watched, or they will soon perish. The hen turkey is so careless, that she will stalk about with one chicken, and leave the remainder, or even tread upon and kill them. Turkeys are violent eaters, and must therefore be left to take charge of themselves in general, except one good feed a day. The hen sets twenty-five or thirty days, and the young ones must be kept warm, as the least cold or damp kills them. They must be fed often, and at a distance from the hen, or she will pick every thing from them. They should have curds, green cheese parings cut small, and bread and milk with chopped wormwood in it. Their drink milk and water, but must not be left to turn sour. All young fowls are a prey for vermin, therefore they should be kept in a safe place where none can come. Weasels, stoats, and ferrets will creep in at a very small crevice. The hen should be under a coop, in a warm place exposed to the sun, for the first three or four weeks; and the young ones should not be suffered to wander about in the dew, at morning or evening. Twelve eggs are enough to put under a turkey; and when she is about to lay, lock her up till she has laid every morning. They usually begin to lay in March, and set in April. Feed them near the hen-house, and give them a little meat in the evening, to accustom them to roosting there. Fatten them with sodden oats or barley for the first fortnight; and the last fortnight give them as above, and rice swelled with warm milk over the fire twice a day. The flesh will be beautifully white and fine flavoured. The common way in Norfolk is to cram them, but they are so ravenous that it seems unnecessary, if they are not suffered to wander far from home, which keeps them lean and poor.—When fat turkeys are to be purchased in the market, in order to judge of their quality it is necessary to observe, that the cock bird when young has a smooth black leg, and a short spur. If fresh and sweet, the eyes are full and bright, and the feet moist and supple. If stale, the eyes will be sunk, and the feet stiff and dry. The hen turkey is known by the same rules; but if old, the legs will be red and rough.

TURKEY PATTIES. Mince some of the white part, and season it with grated lemon, nutmeg, salt, a dust of white pepper, a spoonful of cream, and a very small piece of butter warmed. Fill the patties, and bake them.

TURKEY PIE. Break the bones, and beat the turkey flat on the breast. Lard it with bacon, lay it into a raised crust with some slices of bacon under it, and well seasoned with salt, pepper, nutmeg, whole cloves, and bay leaves. Lay a slice of bacon over it, cover it with a crust, and bake it. When baked, put a clove of garlic or shalot into the whole in the middle of the crust, and let it stand till cold. The turkey may be boned if preferred. Duck or goose pie may be made in the same manner.

TURKEY SAUCE. Open some oysters into a bason, and pour the liquor into a saucepan as soon as it is settled. Add a little white gravy, and a tea-spoonful of lemon pickle. Thicken it with flour and butter, boil it a few minutes, add a spoonful of cream, and then the oysters. Shake them over the fire, but do not let them boil. Or boil some slices or fine bread with a little salt, an onion, and a few peppercorns. Beat it well, put in a bit of butter, and a spoonful of cream. This sauce eats well with roast turkey or veal.

TURKISH YOGURT. Let a small quantity of milk stand till it be sour, then put a sufficient quantity of it to new milk, to turn it to a soft curd. This may be eaten with sugar only, or both this and the fresh cheese are good eaten with strawberries and raspberries, as cream, or with sweetmeats of any kind.

TURNIPS. To dress this valuable root, pare off all the outside coat, cut them in two, and boil them with beef, mutton, or lamb. When they become tender take them up, press away the liquor, and mash them with butter and salt, or send them to table whole, with melted butter in a boat. Young turnips look and eat well with a little of the top left on them. To preserve turnips for the winter, cut off the tops and tails, and leave the roots a few days to dry. They should then be stacked up with layers of straw between, so as to keep them from the rain and frost, and let the stack be pointed at the top.

TURNIPS MASHED. Pare and boil them quite tender, squeeze them as dry as possible between two trenchers, put them into a stewpan, and mash them with a wooden spoon. Then rub them through a cullender, add a little bit of butter, keep stirring them till the butter is melted and well mixed with them, and they are ready for the table.

TURNIP BUTTER. In the fall of the year, butter is apt to acquire a strong and disagreeable flavour, from the cattle feeding on turnips, cabbages, leaves of trees, and other vegetable substances. To correct the offensive taste which this produces, boil two ounces of saltpetre in a quart of water, and put two or more spoonfuls of it into a pail before milking, according to the quantity of milk. If this be done constantly, the evil will be effectually cured: if not, it will be owing to the neglect of the dairy maid.

TURNIP FLY. To prevent the black fly from injuring the turnip crop, mix an ounce of sulphur daily with three pounds of turnip seed for three days successively, and keep it closely covered in an earthen pan. Stir it well each time, that the seed may be duly impregnated with the sulphur. Sow it as usual on an acre of ground, and the fly will not attack it till after the third or fourth leaf be formed, when the plant will be entirely out of danger. If garden vegetables be attacked by the fly, water them freely with a decoction of elder leaves.

TURNIP PIE. Season some mutton chops with salt and pepper, reserving the ends of the neck bones to lay over the turnips, which must be cut into small dice, and put on the steaks. Add two or three spoonfuls of milk, also a sliced onion if approved, and cover with a crust.

TURNIP SAUCE. Pare half a dozen turnips, boil them in a little water, keep them shaking till they are done, and the liquor quite exhausted, and then rub them through a tammis. Take a little white gravy and cut more turnips, as if intended for harrico. Shake them as before, and add a little more white gravy.

TURNIP SOUP. Take from a knuckle of veal all the meat that can be made into cutlets, and stew the remainder in five pints of water, with an onion, a bundle of herbs, and a blade of mace. Cover it close, and let it do on a slow fire, four or five hours at least. Strain it, and set it by till the next day. Then take the fat and sediment from it, and simmer it with turnips cut into small dice till tender, seasoning it with salt and pepper. Before serving, rub down half a spoonful of flour with half a pint of good cream, and a piece of butter the size of a walnut. Let a small roll simmer in the soup till fully moistened, and serve this with it. The soup should be as thick as middling cream.

TURNIP TOPS. These are the shoots which come out in the spring from the old turnip roots, and are to be dressed in the same way as cabbage sprouts. They make very nice sweet greens, and are esteemed great purifiers of the blood and juices.

TURNPIKES. Mix together a quarter of a pound each of flour, butter, currants, and lump sugar powdered. Beat up four eggs with two of the whites, make the whole into a stiff paste, with the addition of a little lemon peel. Roll the paste out thin, and cut it into shapes with a wine glass. The addition of a few carraway seeds will be an improvement.

TURTLE. The morning that you intend to dress the turtle, fill a boiler or kettle with a quantity of water sufficient to scald the callapach and callapee, the fins, &c. and about nine o'clock hang up your turtle by the hind fins, cut off its head, and save the blood; then with a sharp pointed knife separate the callapach from the callapee (or the back from the belly part) down to the shoulders, so as to come at the entrails, which take out, and clean them, as you would those of any other animal, and throw them into a tub of clean water, taking great care not to break the gall, but cut it off the liver, and throw it away. Then separate each distinctly, and take the guts into another vessel, open them with a small penknife, from end to end, wash them clean, and draw them through a woollen cloth in warm water, to clear away the slime, and then put them into clean cold water till they are used, with the other part of the entrails, which must all be cut up small to be mixed in the baking dishes with the meat. This done, separate the back and belly pieces entirely, cutting away the four fins by the upper joint, which scald, peel off the loose skin, and cut them into small pieces, laying them by themselves, either in another vessel, or on the table, ready to be seasoned. Then cut off the meat from the belly part, and clean the back from the lungs, kidneys, &c. and that meat cut into pieces as small as a walnut, laying it likewise by itself. After this you are to scald the back and belly pieces, pulling off the shell from the back and the yellow skin from the belly; when all will be white and clean, and with the kitchen cleaver cut those up likewise into pieces about the bigness or breadth of a card. Put those pieces into clean cold water, wash them out, and place them in a heap on the table, so that each part may lie by itself. The meat, being thus prepared and laid separately for seasoning, mix two third parts of salt, or rather more, and one third part of Cayenne pepper, black pepper, and a spoonful of nutmeg and mace pounded fine, and mixed together; the quantity to be proportioned to the size of the turtle, so that in each dish there may be about three spoonfuls of seasoning to every twelve pounds of meat. Your meat being thus seasoned, get some sweet herbs, such as thyme, savoury, &c. let them be dried and rubbed fine, and having provided some deep dishes to bake it in, (which should be of the common brown ware) put in the coarsest parts of the meat at the bottom, with about a quarter of a pound of butter in each dish, and then some of each of the several parcels of meat, so that the dishes may be all alike, and have equal portions of the different parts of the turtle; and between each laying of the meat, strew a little of this mixture of sweet herbs. Fill your dishes within an inch and an half, or two inches of the top; boil the blood of the turtle, and put into it; then lay on forcemeat balls made of veal, or fowl, highly seasoned with the same seasoning as the turtle; put into each dish a gill of good Madeira wine, and as much water as it will conveniently hold; then break over it five or six eggs, to keep the meat from scorching at the top, and over that shake a small handful of shred parsley, to make it look green; which done, put your dishes into an oven made hot enough to bake bread, and in an hour and half, or two hours, (according to the size of the dishes) it will be sufficiently done. Send it to the table in the dishes in which it is baked, in order to keep it warm while it is eating.

TURTLE FINS. Put into a stewpan five large spoonfuls of brown sauce, with a bottle of port wine, and a quart of mushrooms. When the sauce boils, put in four fins; and after taking away all the small bones that are seen breaking through the skin, add a few sprigs of parsley, a bit of thyme, one bay leaf, and four cloves, and let it simmer one hour. Ten minutes before it is done, put in five dozen of button onions ready peeled, and see that it is properly salted.

    TURTLE SOUP. The best sized turtle is one from sixty to eighty pounds weight, which will make six or eight tureens of fine soup. Kill the turtle the evening before; tie a cord to the hind fins, and hang it up with the head downwards. Tie the fore fins by way of pinioning them, otherwise it would beat itself, and be troublesome to the executioner. Hold the head in the left hand, and with a sharp knife cut off the neck as near the head as possible. Lay the turtle on a block on the back shell, slip the knife between the breast and the edge of the back shell; and when the knife has been round, and the breast is detached from the back, pass the fingers underneath, and detach the breast from the fins, always keeping the edge of the knife on the side of the breast; otherwise if the gall be broken, the turtle will be spoiled. Cut the breast into four pieces, remove the entrails, beginning by the liver, and cut away the gall, to be out of danger at once. When the turtle is emptied, throw the heart, liver, kidneys, and lights, into a large tub of water. Cut away the fins to the root, as near to the back shell as possible; then cut the fins in the second joint, that the white meat may be separated from the green. Scrape the fat from the back shell by skimming it, and put it aside. Cut the back shell into four pieces. Set a large turbot pan on the fire, and when it boils dip a fin into it for a minute, then take it out and peel it very clean. When that is done, take another, and so on till all are done; then the head, next the shell and breast, piece by piece. Be careful to have the peel and shell entirely cleaned off, then put in the same pan some clean water, with the breast and back, the four fins, and the head. Let it boil till the bones will leave the meat, adding a large bundle of turtle herbs, four bay leaves, and some thyme. If two dishes are to be made of the fins, they must be removed when they have boiled one hour. Put into a small stewpan the liver, lights, heart, and kidneys, and the fat that was laid aside. Take some of the liquor that the other part was boiled in, cover the stewpan close, and let it boil gently for three hours. Clean the bones, breast, and back from the green fat, and cut it into pieces an inch long, and half an inch wide, but suffer none of it to be wasted. Put all these pieces on a dish, and set it by till the broth is ready. To prepare the broth, put on a large stockpot, and line the bottom of it with a pound and a half of lean ham, cut into slices. Cut into pieces a large leg of veal, except a pound of the fillet to be reserved for forcemeat; put the rest upon the ham, with all the white meat of the turtle, and a couple of old fowls. Put it on a smart fire, with two ladlefuls of rich broth, and reduce it to a glaze. When it begins to stick to the bottom, pour the liquor in which the turtle was boiled into the pot where the other part of the turtle has been boiled. Add to it a little more sweet herbs, twenty-four grains of allspice, six blades of mace, two large onions, four carrots, half an ounce of whole pepper, and some salt. Let it simmer for four hours, and then strain the broth through a cloth sieve. Put into it the green part of the turtle that has been cut in pieces and nicely cleaned, with two bottles of Madeira. When it has boiled a few minutes with the turtle, add the broth to it. Melt half a pound of butter in a stewpan, add four large spoonfuls of flour, stir it on the fire till of a fine brown colour, and pour some of the broth to it. Mix it well, and strain it through a hair sieve into the soup. Cut the liver, lights, heart, kidneys, and fat into small square pieces, and put them into the soup with half a tea-spoonful of cayenne, two of curry powder, and four table-spoonfuls of the essence of anchovies. Let it boil an hour and a half, carefully skimming off the fat. Pound the reserved veal in a marble mortar for the forcemeat, and rub it through a hair sieve, with as much of the udder as there is of meat from the leg of veal. Put some bread crumbs into a stewpan with milk enough to moisten it, adding a little chopped parsley and shalot. Dry it on the fire, rub it through a wire sieve, and when cold mix it all together, that every part may be equally blended. Boil six eggs hard, take the yolks and pound them with the other ingredients; season it with salt, cayenne, and a little curry powder. Add three raw eggs, mix all well together, and make the forcemeat into small balls the size of a pigeon's egg. Ten minutes before the soup is ready put in the forcemeat balls, and continue to skim the soup till it is taken off the fire. If the turtle weighs eighty pounds, it will require nearly three bottles of Madeira for the soup. When the turtle is dished, squeeze two lemons into each tureen. It is also very good with eggs boiled hard, and a dozen of the yolks put in each tureen. This is a highly fashionable soup, and such as is made in the royal kitchen; but it is difficult of digestion, and fit only for those who 'live to eat.' Foreigners in general are extremely fond of it; and at the Spanish dinner in 1808, eight hundred guests attended, and two thousand five hundred pounds weight of turtle were consumed.

TUSK. Lay the tusk in water the first thing in the morning; after it has lain three or four hours, scale and clean it very well; then shift the water, and let it lie till you want to dress it. If it is large, cut it down the back, and then across; if small, only down the back; put it into cold water, and let it boil gently for about twenty minutes. Send it to table in a napkin, with egg sauce, butter and mustard, and parsnips cut in slices, in a plate.

TWOPENNY. The malt beverage thus denominated, is not formed to keep, and therefore not likely to be brewed by any persons for their own consumption. The following proportions for one barrel, are inserted merely to add to general information in the art of brewing.

	£	s.	d.
Malt, a bushel and a half	0	9	0
Hops, one pound	0	1	6
Liquorice root, a pound and a half	0	1	6
Capsicum, a quarter of an ounce	0	0	1
Spanish liquorice, 2 ounces	0	0	2
Treacle, five pounds	0	1	8
	0	13	11

	£	s.	d.
One barrel of twopenny, paid for at the publican's, 128 quarts, at *4d.* per quart	2	2	8
Brewed at home, coals included	0	15	0
Clear gain,	1	7	8

It is sufficient to observe respecting this liquor, that it requires no storing, being frequently brewed one week, and consumed the next. The quantity of capsicum in one barrel of twopenny, is as much as is commonly contained in two barrels of porter: this readily accounts for the preference given to it by the working classes, in cold winter mornings. Twopenny works remarkably quick, and must be carefully attended to, in the barrels.

VACCINE INOCULATION. One of the most important discoveries in the history of animal nature is that of the Cow Pox, which was publicly announced by Dr. Jenner in the year 1798, though it had for ages been known by some of the dairymen in the west of England. This malady appears on the nipples of cows in the form of irregular pustules, and it is now ascertained that persons inoculated with the matter taken from them are thereby rendered incapable of the small pox infection. Innumerable experiments have been made in different countries, in Asia and America, with nearly the same success; and by a series of facts duly authenticated, in many thousands of instances, it is fully proved that the vaccine inoculation is a milder and safer disease than the inoculated small pox; and while the one has saved its tens of thousands, the other is going on to save its millions. With a view of extending the beneficial effects of the new inoculation to the poor, a new dispensary, called the Vaccine Institution, has been established in London, where the operation is performed gratis, and the vaccine matter may be had by those who wish to promote this superior method of inoculation. The practice itself is very simple. Nothing more is necessary than making a small puncture in the skin of the arm, and applying the matter. But as it is of great consequence that the matter be good, and not too old, it is recommended to apply for the assistance of those who make it a part of their business, as the expense is very trifling.

VARNISH FOR BOOTS. To render boots and shoes impervious to the wet, take a pint of linseed oil, half a pound of mutton suet, six or eight ounces of bees' wax, and a small piece of rosin. Boil all together in a pipkin, and let it cool to milk warm. Then with a hair brush lay it on new boots or shoes; but it is better still to lay it on the leather before the articles are made. The shoes or boots should also be brushed over with it, after they come from the maker. If old boots or shoes are to be varnished, the mixture is to be laid on when the leather is perfectly dry.

VARNISH FOR BRASS. Put into a pint of alcohol, an ounce of turmeric powder, two drams of arnatto, and two drams of saffron. Agitate the mixture during seven days, and filter it into a clean bottle. Now add three ounces of clean seed-lac, and agitate the bottle every day for fourteen days. When the lacquer is used, the pieces of brass if large are to be first warmed, so as to heat the hand, and the varnish is to be applied with a brush. Smaller pieces may be dipped in the varnish, and then drained by holding them for a minute over the bottle. This varnish, when applied to rails for desks, has a most beautiful appearance, like that of burnished gold.

VARNISH FOR DRAWINGS. Mix together two ounces of spirits of turpentine, and one ounce of Canada balsam. The print is first to be sized with a solution of isinglass water, and dried; the varnish is then to be applied with a camel-hair brush. But for oil paintings, a different composition is prepared. A small piece of white sugar candy is dissolved and mixed with a spoonful of brandy; the whites of eggs are then beaten to a froth, and the clear part is poured off and incorporated with the mixture. The paintings are then brushed over with the varnish, which is easily washed off when they are required to be cleaned again, and on this account it will be far superior to any other kind of varnish for this purpose.

VARNISH FOR FANS. To make a varnish for fans and cases, dissolve two ounces of gum-mastic, eight ounces of gum-sandaric, in a quart of alcohol, and then add four ounces of Venice turpentine.

VARNISH FOR FIGURES. Fuse in a crucible half an ounce of tin, with the same quantity of bismuth. When melted, add half an ounce of mercury; and when perfectly combined, take the mixture from the fire and cool it. This substance, mixed with the white of an egg, forms a very beautiful varnish for plaster figures.

VARNISH FOR FURNITURE. This is made of white wax melted in the oil of petrolium. A light coat of this mixture is laid on the wood with a badger's brush, while a little warm, and the oil will speedily evaporate. A coat of wax will be left behind, which should afterwards be polished with a woollen cloth.

VARNISH FOR HATS. The shell of the hat having been prepared, dyed, and formed in the usual manner, is to be stiffened, when perfectly dry, with the following composition, worked upon the inner surface. One pound of gum kino, eight ounces of gum elemi, three pounds of gum olibanum, three pounds of gum copal, two pounds of gum juniper, one pound of gum ladanum, one pound of gum mastic, ten pounds of shell lac, and eight ounces of frankincense. These are pounded small and mixed together; three gallons of alcohol are then placed in an earthen vessel to receive the pounded gums, and the vessel is then to be frequently agitated. When the gums are sufficiently dissolved by this process, a pint of liquid ammonia is added to the mixture, with an ounce of oil of lavender, and a pound of gum myrrh and gum opoponax, dissolved in three pints of spirit of wine. The whole of the ingredients being perfectly incorporated and free from lumps, constitute the patent water-proof mixture with which the shell of the hat is stiffened. When the shell has been dyed, shaped, and rendered perfectly dry, its inner surface and the under side of the brim are varnished with this composition by means of a brush. The hat is then placed in a warm drying-room until it becomes hard. This process is repeated several times, taking care that the varnish does not penetrate through the shell, so as to appear on the outside. To allow the perspiration of the head to evaporate, small holes are to be pierced through the crown of the hat from the inside outward; and the nap of silk, beaver, or other fur, is to be laid on by the finisher in the usual way. That on the under side of the brim, which has been prepared as above, is to be attached with copal varnish.

VARNISH FOR PAINTINGS. Mix six ounces of pure mastic gum with the same quantity of pounded glass, and introduce the compound into a bottle containing a pint of oil of turpentine. Now add half an ounce of camphor bruised in a mortar. When the mastic is dissolved, put in an ounce of Venice turpentine, and agitate the whole till the turpentine is perfectly dissolved. When the varnish is to be applied to oil paintings, it must be gently poured from the glass sediment, or filtered through a muslin.

VARNISH FOR PALING. A varnish for any kind of coarse wood work is made of tar ground up with Spanish brown, to the consistence of common paint, and then spread on the wood with a large brush as soon as made, to prevent its growing too stiff and hard. The colour may be changed by mixing a little white lead, whiting, or ivory black, with the Spanish brown. For pales and weather boards this varnish is superior to paint, and much cheaper than what is commonly used for that purpose. It is an excellent preventive against wet and weather, and if laid on smooth wood it will have a good gloss.

VARNISH FOR SILKS. To one quart of cold-drawn linseed oil, add half an ounce of litharge. Boil them for half an hour, and then add half an ounce of copal varnish. While the ingredients are heating in a copper vessel, put in one ounce of rosin, and a few drops of neatsfoot oil, stirring the whole together with a knife. When cool, it is ready for use. This varnish will set, or keep its place on the silk in four hours, the silk may then be turned and varnished on the other side.

VARNISH FOR STRAW HATS. For straw or chip hats, put half an ounce of black sealing-wax powdered into two ounces of spirits of wine or turpentine, and place it near the fire till the wax is dissolved. If the hat has lost its colour or turned brown, it may first be brushed over with writing ink, and well dried. The varnish is then to be laid on warm with a soft brush, in the sun or before the fire, and it will give it a new gloss which will resist the wet.

VARNISH FOR TINWARE. Put three ounces of seed-lac, two drams of dragon's blood, and one ounce of turmeric powder, into a pint of well-rectified spirits. Let the whole remain for fourteen days, but during that time, agitate the bottle once a day at least. When properly combined, strain the liquid through a piece of muslin. This varnish is called lacquer; it is brushed over tinware to give it a resemblance to brass.

VARNISH FOR WOOD. The composition which is the best adapted to preserve wood from the decay occasioned both by the wet and the dry rot, is as follows. Melt twelve ounces of rosin in an iron kettle, and when melted, add eight ounces of roll brimstone. When both are in a liquid state, pour in three gallons of train oil. Heat the whole slowly, gradually adding four ounces of bees' wax in small pieces, and keep the mixture stirring. As soon as the solid ingredients are dissolved, add as much Spanish brown, red or yellow ochre, ground fine with some of the oil, as will give the whole a deep shade. Lay on this varnish as hot and thin as possible; and some days after the first coat becomes dry, give a second. This will preserve planks and other wood for ages.

VEAL. In purchasing this article, the following things should be observed. The flesh of a bull calf is the firmest, but not so white. The fillet of the cow calf is generally preferred for the udder. The whitest meat is not the most juicy, having been made so by frequent bleeding, and giving the calf some whiting to lick. Choose that meat which has the kidney well covered with fat, thick and white. If the bloody vein in the shoulder look blue, or of a bright red, it is newly killed; but any other colour shows it stale. The other parts should be dry and white: if clammy or spotted, the meat is stale and bad. The kidney turns first in the loin, and the suet will not then be firm. This should carefully be attended to, if the joint is to be kept a little time. The first part that turns bad in a leg of veal, is where the udder is skewered back: of course the skewer should be taken out, and both that and the part under it wiped every day. It will then keep good three or four days in hot weather. Take care also to cut out the pipe that runs along the chine of a loin of veal, the same as in beef, to hinder it from tainting. The skirt of the breast of veal is likewise to be taken off, and the inside of the breast wiped and scraped, and sprinkled with a little salt.

VEAL BLANQUETS. Cut thin slices off a fillet of veal roasted. Put some butter into a stewpan, with an onion chopped small; fry them till they begin to brown, then dust in some flour, and add some gravy, and a faggot of sweet herbs, seasoned with pepper, salt, and mace; let this simmer till you have the flavour of the herbs, then put in your veal; beat up the yolks of two eggs in a little cream, and grated nutmeg, some chopped parsley, and a little lemon peel shred fine. Keep it stirring one way till it is smooth, and of a good thickness: squeeze in a little juice of orange, and dish it up. Garnish with orange and barberries.

VEAL BROTH. To make a very nourishing veal broth, take off the knuckle of a leg or shoulder of veal, with very little meat to it, and put it into a stewpot, with three quarts of water. Add an old fowl, four shank-bones of mutton extremely well soaked and bruised, three blades of mace, ten peppercorns, an onion, and a large slice of bread. Cover it close, boil it up once, and skim it carefully. Simmer it four hours as slowly as possible, strain and take off the fat, and flavour it with a little salt.—Another way. Take a scrag of veal, of about three pounds; put it into a clean saucepan, with a tea-spoonful of salt; when it boils, scum it clean; put in a spoonful of ground rice, some mace, a faggot of herbs, and let it boil gently for near two hours, or till you have about two quarts: send it to table with your veal in the middle, toasted bread, and parsley and butter in a boat.

VEAL A LA CREME. Take the best end of a loin of veal, joint it, and cut a little of the suet from the kidney. Make it lie flat, then cut a place in the middle of the upper part about three inches deep and six inches long, take the piece out and chop it, add a little beef suet or beef marrow, parsley, thyme, green truffles, mushrooms, shalots, lemon peel chopped fine, and season it with pepper, salt, and a little beaten allspice. Put all together into a marble mortar, add the yolks of two eggs, and a little French bread soaked in cream. Pound the ingredients well, fill the cavity with the forcemeat, and cover it with a piece of veal caul. Then tie it down close, cover the whole with a large piece of caul, and roast it gently. When to be served up, take off the large caul, let it colour a little, glaze it lightly, and put under it a white sauce. A fillet of veal may be done in the same way, instead of using plain stuffing for it.

VEAL CAKE. Boil six or eight eggs hard; cut the yolks in two, and lay some of the pieces in the bottom of the pot. Shake in a little chopped parsley, some slices of veal and ham, and then eggs again; shaking in after each, some chopped parsley, with pepper and salt, till the pot is full. Then put in water enough to cover it, and lay on it about an ounce of butter: tie it over with a double paper, and bake it about an hour. Then press it close together with a spoon, and let it stand till cold. The cake may be put into a small mould, and then it will turn out beautifully for a supper or side dish.

VEAL COLLOPS. Cut long thin collops, beat them well, and lay on them a bit of thin bacon of the same size. Spread forcemeat over, seasoned high, and also a little garlic and cayenne. Roll them up tight, about the size of two fingers, but not more than two or three inches long. Fasten each firmly with a small skewer, smear them over with egg, fry them of a fine brown, and pour a rich brown gravy over.—To dress collops quickly in another way, cut them as thin as paper, and in small bits, with a very sharp knife. Throw the skin and any odd bits of veal into a little water, with a dust of pepper and salt. Set them on the fire while the collops are preparing and beating, and dip them into a seasoning of herbs, bread, pepper, salt, and a scrape of nutmeg, having first wetted them with egg. Then put a bit of butter into a fryingpan, and give the collops a very quick fry; for as they are so thin, two minutes will do them on both sides. Put them into a hot dish before the fire, strain and thicken the gravy, give it a boil in the fryingpan, and pour it over the collops. The addition of a little ketchup will be an improvement.—Another way is to fry the collops in butter, seasoned only with salt and pepper. Then simmer them in gravy, either white or brown, with bits of bacon served with them. If white, add lemon peel and mace, and a little cream.

VEAL CUTLETS. Cut the veal into thin slices, dip them in the yolks of egg, strew them over with grated bread and nutmeg, sweet herbs and parsley, and lemon peel minced fine, and fry them with butter. When the meat is done, lay it on a dish before the fire. Put a little water into the pan, stir it round and let it boil; add a little butter rolled in flour, and a little lemon juice, and pour it over the cutlets. Or fry them without the bread and herbs, boil a little flour and water in the pan with a sprig of thyme, and pour it on the cutlets, but take out the thyme before the dish is sent to table.

VEAL GRAVY. Make it as for cullis; but leave out the spices, herbs, and flour. It should be drawn very slowly; and if for white dishes, the meat should not be browned.

VEAL LARDED. Take off the under bone of a neck of veal, and leave only a part of the long bones on. Trim it neatly, lard and roast it gently with a veal caul over it. Ten minutes before it is done, take off the caul, and let the veal be of a very light colour. When it is to be served up, put under it some sorrel sauce, celery heads, or asparagus tops, or serve it with mushroom sauce.

VEAL OLIVES. Cut some long thin collops, beat them, lay them on thin slices of fat bacon, and over these a layer of forcemeat highly seasoned, with some shred shalot and cayenne. Roll them tight, about the size of two fingers, but not more than two or three inches long. Fasten them round with a small skewer, rub egg over them, and fry them of a light brown. Serve with brown gravy, in which boil some mushrooms pickled or fresh, and garnish with fried balls.

VEAL OLIVE PIE. Having prepared the veal olives, lay them round and round the dish, making them highest in the middle. Fill it nearly up with water, and cover it with paste. When baked, mix some gravy, cream, and flour, and pour it hot into the pie.

VEAL PATTIES. Mince some veal that is not quite done, with a little parsley, lemon peel, a dust of salt and nutmeg. Add a spoonful of cream, gravy sufficient to moisten the meat, and a little scraped ham. This mixture is not to be warmed till the patties are baked.

VEAL PIE. Take some of the middle or scrag of a small neck, and season it, adding or not a few slices of lean bacon or ham. If wanted of a high relish, add mace, cayenne, and nutmeg, to the salt and pepper; also forcemeat, and eggs. To these likewise may be added, truffles, morels, mushrooms, sweetbreads cut into small bits, and cocks' combs blanched, if approved. It will be very good without any of the latter additions, but a rich gravy must be prepared, and poured in after baking.—To make a rich veal pie, cut steaks from a neck or breast of veal, season them with pepper, salt, nutmeg, and a very little clove in powder. Slice two sweetbreads, and season them in the same manner. Lay a puff paste on the ledge of the dish, put in the meat, yolks of hard eggs, the sweetbreads, and some oysters, up to the top of the dish. Lay over the whole some very thin slices of ham, and fill up the dish with water. Cover it with a crust, and when taken out of the oven, pour in at the top, through a funnel, a few spoonfuls of good veal gravy, and fill it up with cream; but first boil and thicken it with a tea-spoonful of flour.

VEAL AND PARSLEY PIE. Cut some slices from a leg or neck of veal; if the leg, from about the knuckle. Season them with salt, scald some pickled parsley, and squeeze it dry. Cut the parsley a little, and lay it at the bottom of the dish; then put in the meat, and so on, in layers. Fill up the dish with new milk, but not so high as to touch the crust. When baked, pour out a little of the milk, and put in half a pint of good scalded cream. Chicken may be cut up, skinned, and dressed in the same way.

VEAL PORCUPINE. Bone a fine large breast of veal, and rub it over with the yolks of two eggs. Spread it out, and lay on it a few slices of bacon, cut as thin as possible. Add a handful of parsley shred fine, the yolks of five eggs, boiled hard and chopped, and a little lemon peel finely shred. Steep the crumb of a penny loaf in cream, and add to it, seasoning the whole together with salt, pepper, and nutmeg. Roll the veal close, and skewer it up. Cut some fat bacon, the lean of boiled ham, and pickled cucumbers, about two inches long. Place these in rows upon the veal, first the ham, then the bacon, and last the cucumbers, till the whole is larded. Put the meat into a deep earthen pan with a pint of water, cover it close, and set it in a slow oven for two hours. Skim off the fat afterwards, and strain the gravy through a sieve into a stewpan. Add a glass of white wine, a little lemon pickle and caper liquor, and a spoonful of mushroom ketchup, and thicken the gravy with a bit of butter rolled in flour. Lay the porcupine on a dish, and pour the sauce over it. Have ready prepared a thin forcemeat, made of the crumb of a penny loaf, half a pound of beef suet shred fine, the yolks of four eggs, and a few oysters chopped. Mix these together, season the forcemeat with cayenne, salt, pepper, and nutmeg, and spread it on the veal caul. Having rolled the whole up tight, like collared eel, bind it in a cloth, and boil it an hour. When done enough, cut it into four slices, laying one at each end, and the others on the sides of the dish. Have the sweetbreads ready prepared, cut in slices and fried, and lay them round the dish, with a few mushrooms pickled. This is allowed to make a fine bottom dish, when game is not to be had.

VEAL ROLLS. Cut thin slices of either fresh or cold veal, spread on them a fine seasoning of a very few crumbs, a little chopped bacon or scraped ham, and a little suet, parsley, and shalot. Or instead of the parsley and shalot, some fresh mushrooms stewed and minced. Then add pepper and salt, and a small piece of pounded mace. This stuffing may either fill up the roll like a sausage, or be rolled with the meat. In either case tie it up very tight, and stew very slowly in good gravy, and a glass of sherry. Skim it very carefully, and serve it up quite tender.—Another way. Take slices of veal, enough to make a side dish; lay them on your dresser, and lay forcemeat upon each slice; roll them up, and tie them round with coarse thread. Rub them over with the yolk of an egg, spit them on a bird spit, and roast them of a fine brown. For sauce, have good gravy, with morels, truffles, and mushrooms, tossed up to a proper thickness. Lay your rolls in your dish, and pour your sauce over. Garnish with lemon.

VEAL SAUSAGES. Chop equal quantities of lean veal and fat bacon, a handful of sage, a little salt and pepper, and a few anchovies. Beat all in a mortar; and when used, roll and fry it. Serve it with fried sippets, or on stewed vegetables, or on white collops.

VEAL SCALLOPS. Mince some cold veal very small, and set it over the fire with a scrape of nutmeg, a little pepper and salt, and a little cream. Heat it for a few minutes, then put it into the scallop shells, and fill them with crumbs of bread. Lay on some pieces of butter, and brown the scallops before the fire. Either veal or chicken looks and eats well, prepared in this way, and lightly covered with crumbs of fried bread; or these may be laid on in little heaps.

VEAL-SUET PUDDING. Cut the crumb of a threepenny loaf into slices, boil and sweeten two quarts of new milk, and pour over it. When soaked, pour out a little of the milk; mix it with six eggs well beaten, and half a nutmeg. Lay the slices of bread into a dish, with layers of currants and veal suet shred, a pound of each. Butter the dish well, and bake it; or if preferred, boil the pudding in a bason.

VEAL SWEETBREAD. Parboil a fine fresh sweetbread for five minutes, and throw it into a basin of water. When the sweetbread is cold, dry it thoroughly in a cloth, and roast it plain. Or beat up the yolk of an egg, and prepare some fine bread crumbs. Run a lark spit or a skewer through it, and tie it on the ordinary spit. Egg it over with a paste brush, powder it well with bread crumbs, and roast it. Serve it up with fried bread crumbs round it, and melted butter, with a little mushroom ketchup and lemon juice. Or serve the sweetbread on toasted bread, garnished with egg sauce or gravy. Instead of spitting the sweetbread, it may be done in a Dutch oven, or fried.

VEGETABLES. There is nothing in which the difference between an elegant and an ordinary table is more visible, than in the dressing of vegetables, especially greens. They may be equally as fine at first, at one place as at another, but their look and taste afterwards are very different, owing entirely to the careless manner in which they have been prepared. Their appearance at table however is not all that should be considered; for though it is certainly desirable that they should be pleasing to the eye, it is of still greater consequence that their best qualities should be carefully preserved. Vegetables are generally a wholesome diet, but become very prejudicial if not properly dressed. Cauliflowers, and others of the same species, are often boiled only crisp, to preserve their beauty. For the look alone, they had better not be boiled at all, and almost as well for the purpose of food, as in such a crude state they are scarcely digestible by the strongest stomach. On the other hand, when overboiled they become vapid, and in a state similar to decay, in which they afford no sweet purifying juices to the stomach, but load it with a mass of mere feculent matter. The same may be said of many other vegetables, their utility being too often sacrificed to appearance, and sent to table in a state not fit to be eaten. A contrary error often prevails respecting potatoes, as if they could never be done too much. Hence they are popped into the saucepan or steamer, just when it happens to suit, and are left doing, not for the time they require, but till it is convenient to take them up; when perhaps their nutricious qualities are all boiled away, and they taste of nothing but water. Ideas of nicety and beauty in this case ought all to be subservient to utility; for what is beauty in vegetables growing in the garden is not so at table, from the change of circumstances. They are brought to be eaten, and if not adapted properly to the occasion, they are deformities on the dish instead of ornaments. The true criterion of beauty is their suitableness to the purposes intended. Let them be carefully adapted to this, by being neither under nor over done, and they will not fail to please both a correct eye and taste, while they constitute a wholesome species of diet. A most pernicious method of dressing vegetables is often adopted, by putting copper into the saucepan with them in the form of halfpence. This is a dangerous experiment, as the green colour imparted by the copperas, renders them in the highest degree unwholesome, and even poisonous. Besides, it is perfectly unnecessary, for if put into boiling water with a little salt, and boiled up directly, they will be as beautifully green as the most fastidious person can require. A little pearlash might safely be used on such an occasion, and with equal effect, its alkaline properties tending to correct the acidity. Many vegetables are more wholesome, and more agreeable to the taste, when stewed a good while, only care must be taken that they stew merely, without being suffered to boil. Boiling produces a sudden effect, stewing a slower effect, and both have their appropriate advantages. But if preparations which ought only to stew, are permitted to boil, the process is destroyed, and a premature effect produced, that cannot be corrected by any future stewing. In order to have vegetables in the best state for the table, they should be gathered in their proper season, when they are in the greatest perfection, and that is when they are most plentiful. Forced vegetables seldom attain their true flavour, as is evident from very early asparagus, which is altogether inferior to that which is matured by nature and common culture, or the mere operation of the sun and climate. Peas and Potatoes are seldom worth eating before midsummer; unripe vegetables being as insipid and unwholesome as unripe fruit, and are liable to the same objections as when they are destroyed by bad cooking. Vegetables are too commonly treated with a sort of cold distrust, as if they were natural enemies. They are seldom admitted freely at our tables, and are often tolerated only upon a sideboard in small quantities, as if of very inferior consideration. The effect of this is like that of all indiscriminate reserve, that we may negatively be said to lose friends, because we have not the confidence to make them. From the same distrust or prejudice, there are many vegetables never used at all, which are nevertheless both wholesome and palatable, particularly amongst those best known under the denomination of herbs. The freer use of vegetable diet would be attended with a double advantage, that of improving our health, and lessening the expense of the table. Attention should however be paid to their size and quality, in order to enjoy them in their highest degree of perfection. The middle size are generally to be preferred to the largest or the smallest; they are more tender, and full of flavour, just before they are quite full grown. Freshness is their chief value and excellence, and the eye easily discovers whether they have been kept too long, as in that case they lose all their verdure and beauty. Roots, greens, salads, and the various productions of the garden, when first gathered, are plump and firm, and have a fragrant freshness which no art can restore, when they have lost it by long keeping, though it will impart a little freshness to put them into cold spring water for some time before they are dressed. They should neither be so young as not to have acquired their good qualities, nor so old as to be on the point of losing them. To boil them in soft water will best preserve the colour of such as are green; or if only hard water be at hand, a tea-spoonful of potash should be added. Great care should be taken to pick and cleanse them thoroughly from dust, dirt, and insects, and nicely to trim off the outside leaves. If allowed to soak awhile in water a little salted, it will materially assist in cleansing them from insects. All the utensils employed in dressing vegetables should be extremely clean and nice; and if any copper vessel is ever used for the purpose, the greatest attention must be paid to its being well tinned. The scum which arises from vegetables as they boil should be carefully removed, as cleanliness is essential both to their looking and eating well. The lid of the saucepan should always be taken off when they boil, to give access to the air, even if it is not otherwise thought necessary. Put in the vegetables when the water boils, with a little salt, and let them boil quickly; when they sink to the bottom, they are generally done enough. Take them up immediately, or they will lose their colour and goodness. Drain the water from them thoroughly, before they are sent to table. When greens are quite fresh gathered, they will not require so much boiling by at least a third of the time, as when they have been gathered a day or two and brought to the public market. The following table shows when the various kinds of vegetables are in season, or the time of their earliest natural growth, and when they are most plentiful, or in their highest perfection.

Artichokes, July, September,
---- Jerusalem ditto, Sept. November,
Angelica stalks, May, June,
Asparagus, April, June,
Beet roots, Dec. January,
Boricole, November, January
Cabbage, May, July,
---- Red ditto, July, August,
---- White ditto, October,
Cardoons, Nov. December,
Carrots, May, August,
Cauliflowers, June, August,
Celery, Sept. November,
Chervil, March, May,
Corn Salad, May, June,
Cucumbers, July, September,
Endive, June, October,
Kidney Beans, July, August,
Leeks, Sept. December,
Lettuce, April, July,
Onions, August, November,
Parsley, February, March,
Parsnips, July, October,
Peas, June, August,

Potatoes, June, November,
Radishes, March, June,
---- Spanish ditto, August, September,
Scarlet Beans, July, August,
Small Salad, May, June,
Salsify, July, August,
Scorzonera, July, August,
Sea Kale, April, May,
Shalots, August, October,
Savory Cabbage, Sept. November,
Sorrel, June, July,
Spinage, March, July,
---- Winter ditto, Oct. November,
Turnips, May, July,
Turnip tops, April, May,
Windsor Beans, June, August.

VEGETABLES AND FISH. Pick, wash, and chop some sorrel, spinage, small onions or chives, and parsley. Put them into a stewpan with fresh butter, a good spoonful of lemon or Seville orange juice, or vinegar and water, some essence of anchovy, and cayenne pepper. Do these gently over the fire till the vegetables are tender, then put in the fish, and stew them till well done.

VEGETABLE ESSENCES. The flavour of the various sweet and savoury herbs may be obtained, by combining their essential oils with rectified spirit of wine, in the proportion of one dram of the former to two ounces of the latter; by picking the leaves, and laying them in a warm place to dry, and then filling a wide-mouth bottle with them, and pouring on them wine, brandy, or vinegar, and letting them steep for fourteen days.

VEGETABLE MARROW. Take off all the skin of six or eight gourds, put them into a stewpan with water, salt, lemon juice, and a bit of butter, or fat bacon. Let them stew gently till quite tender, and serve them up with rich Dutch sauce, or any other sauce highly flavoured.

VEGETABLE PIE. Scald and blanch some broad beans, and cut in some young carrots, turnips, artichoke bottoms, mushrooms, peas, onions, parsley, celery, or any of these. Make the whole into a nice stew, with some good veal gravy. Bake a crust over a dish, with a little lining round the edge, and a cup turned up to keep it from sinking. When baked, open the lid, and pour in the stew.

VEGETABLE SOUP. Pare and slice five or six cucumbers, add the inside of as many cos-lettuces, a sprig or two of mint, two or three onions, some pepper and salt, a pint and a half of young peas, and a little parsley. Put these into a saucepan with half a pound of fresh butter, to stew in their own liquor half an hour, near a gentle fire. Pour on the vegetables two quarts of boiling water, and stew them two hours. Rub a little flour in a tea-cupful of water, boil it with the rest nearly twenty minutes, and serve it.—Another way. Peel and slice six large onions, six potatoes, six carrots, and four turnips; fry them in half a pound of butter, and pour on them four quarts of boiling water. Toast a crust of bread quite brown and hard, but do not burn it; add it to the above, with some celery, sweet herbs, white pepper, and salt. Stew it all together gently four hours, and strain it through a coarse cloth. Put in a sliced carrot, some celery, and a small turnip, and stew them in the soup. An anchovy, and a spoonful of ketchup, may be added if approved.

VEGETABLE SYRUP. To a pint of white wine vinegar, put two pounds of the best brown sugar. Boil them to a syrup; and when quite cold, add two table-spoonfuls of paregoric elixir, which is made in the following manner. Steep in a pint of brandy a dram of purified opium, a dram of flowers of benjamin, and two scruples of camphor, adding a dram of the oil of anniseed. Let it stand ten days, occasionally shaking it up, and then strain it off. This added to the above composition, forms the celebrated Godbold's Vegetable Syrup. The paregoric elixir taken by itself, a tea-spoonful in half a pint of white wine whey or gruel at bed time, is an agreeable and effectual medicine for coughs and colds. It is also excellent for children who have the hooping cough, in doses of from five to twenty drops in a little water, or on a small piece of sugar. The vegetable syrup is chiefly intended for consumptive cases.

VELVETS. When the pile of velvet requires to be raised, it is only necessary to warm a smoothing iron, to cover it with a wet cloth, and hold it under the velvet. The vapour arising from the wet cloth will raise the pile of the velvet, with the assistance of a whisk gently passed over it. To remove spots and stains in velvet, bruise some of the plant called soapwort, strain out the juice, and add to it a small quantity of black soap. Wash the stain with this liquor, and repeat it several times after it has been allowed to dry. To take wax out of velvet, rub it frequently with hot toasted bread.

VENISON. If it be young and good, the fat of the venison will be clear, bright, and thick, and the cleft part smooth and close: but if the cleft is wide and tough, it is old. To judge of its sweetness, run a very sharp narrow knife into the shoulder or haunch, and the meat will be known by the scent. Few people like it when it is very high.

VENISON PASTY. To prepare venison for pasty, take out all the bones, beat and season the meat, and lay it into a stone jar in large pieces. Pour over it some plain drawn beef gravy, not very strong; lay the bones on the top, and set the jar in a water bath, or saucepan of water over the fire, and let it simmer three or four hours. The next day, when quite cold, remove the cake of fat, and lay the meat in handsome pieces on the dish. If not sufficiently seasoned, add more pepper, salt, or pimento. Put in some of the gravy, and keep the remainder for the time of serving. When the venison is thus prepared, it will not require so much time to bake, or such a very thick crust as usual, and by which the under part is seldom done through. A shoulder of venison makes a good pasty, and if there be a deficiency of fat, it must be supplied from a good loin of mutton, steeped twenty-four hours in equal parts of rape, vinegar, and port. The shoulder being sinewy, it will be of advantage to rub it well with sugar for two or three days; and when to be used, clear it perfectly from the sugar and the wine with a dry cloth. A mistake used to prevail, that venison could not be baked too much; but three or four hours in a slow oven will be sufficient to make it tender, and the flavour will be preserved. Whether it be a shoulder or a side of venison, the meat must be cut in pieces, and laid with fat between, that it may be proportioned to each person, without breaking up the pasty to find it. Lay some pepper and salt at the bottom of the dish, and some butter; then the meat nicely packed, that it may be sufficiently done, but not lie hollow to harden at the edges. In order to provide gravy for the pasty, boil the venison bones with some fine old mutton, and put half a pint of the gravy cold into the dish. Then lay butter on the venison and cover as well as line the sides with a thick crust, but none must be put under the meat. Keep the remainder of the gravy till the pasty comes from the oven; pour it quite hot into the middle by means of a funnel, and mix it well in the dish by shaking. It should be seasoned with pepper and salt.—Another way. Take a side of venison, bone it, and season it with pepper and salt, cloves, and mace finely beaten; cut your venison in large pieces, and season it very well with your spices then lay it into an earthen pan; make a good gravy of two pound of beef, and pour this gravy over the venison; take three quarters of a pound of beef suet, well picked from the skins, wet a coarse cloth, lay your suet on it, and cover it over, and beat it with a rolling-pin, till it is as fine as butter; as your cloth dries, wet it, and shift your suet, and put it over the top of the venison; make a paste of flour and water, and cover the pan, and send it to the oven to bake; it is best baked with a batch of bread; when it comes from the oven, and is quite cold, make a puff-paste; lay a paste all over your dish, and a roll round the inside, then put in your venison with the fat, and all the gravy, if the dish will hold it; put on the lid, and ornament it as your fancy leads. It will take two hours and a half in a quick oven. A sheet of paper laid on the top, will prevent it from catching, and the crust will be of a fine colour. By baking your venison in this manner, it will keep four or five days before you use it, if you do not take off the crust.

VENISON SAUCE. Boil an ounce of dried currants in half a pint of water, and some crumbs of bread, a few cloves or grated nutmeg, a glass of port wine, and a piece of butter. Sweeten it to your taste, and send it to table in a boat.

VERJUICE. Lay some ripe crabs together in a heap to sweat, then take out the stalks and decayed ones, and mash up the rest. Press the juice through a hair cloth into a clean vessel, and it will be fit to use in a month. It is proper for sauces where lemon is wanted.

VERMICELLI PUDDING. Boil a pint of milk with lemon peel and cinnamon, and sweeten it with loaf sugar. Strain it through a sieve, add a quarter of a pound of vermicelli, and boil it ten minutes. Then put in the yolks of five and the whites of three eggs, mix them well together, and steam the pudding an hour and a quarter, or bake it half an hour.

VERMICELLI SOUP. Boil two ounces of vermicelli in three quarts of veal gravy, then rub it through a tammis, season it with salt, give it a boil, and skim it well. Beat up the yolks of four eggs, mix with them half a pint of cream, stir them gradually into the soup, simmer it for a few minutes, and serve it up. A little of the vermicelli may be reserved to serve in the soup, if approved.—Another way. Take two quarts of strong veal broth, put into a clean saucepan a piece of bacon stuck with cloves, and half an ounce of butter worked up in flour; then take a small fowl trussed to boil, break the breastbone, and put it into your soup; stove it close, and let it stew three quarters of an hour; take about two ounces of vermicelli, and put to it some of the broth; set it over the fire till it is quite tender. When your soup is ready, take out the fowl, and put it into your dish; take out your bacon, skim your soup as clean as possible; then pour it on the fowl, and lay your vermicelli all over it; cut some French bread thin, put it into your soup, and send it to table. If you chuse it, you may make your soup with a knuckle of veal, and send a handsome piece of it in the middle of your dish, instead of the fowl.

VICARAGE CAKE. Mix a pound and a half of fine flour, half a pound of moist sugar, a little grated nutmeg and ginger, two eggs well beaten, a table-spoonful of yeast, and the same of brandy. Make it into a light paste, with a quarter of a pound of butter melted in half a pint of milk. Let it stand half an hour before the fire to rise, then add three quarters of a pound of currants, well washed and cleaned, and bake the cake in a brisk oven. Butter the tin before the cake is put into it.

VINEGAR. Allow a pound of lump sugar to a gallon of water. While it is boiling, skim it carefully, and pour it into a tub to cool. When it is no more than milk warm, rub some yeast upon a piece of bread and put into it, and let it ferment about twenty-four hours. Then tun the liquor into a cask with iron hoops, lay a piece of tile over the bung-hole, and set it in the kitchen, which is better than placing it in the sun. It will be fit to bottle in about six months. March is the best time of the year for making vinegar, though if kept in the kitchen, this is of less consequence. A cheap sort of vinegar may be made of the refuse of the bee hives, after the honey is extracted. Put the broken combs into a vessel, and add two parts of water: expose it to the sun, or keep it in a warm place. Fermentation will succeed in a few days, when it must be well stirred and pressed down to make it soak; and when the fermentation is over, the matter is to be laid upon sieves to drain. The yellow liquor which forms at the bottom of the vessel must be removed, the vessel well cleaned, and the liquor which has been strained is to be returned to the vessel. It will immediately begin to turn sour; it should therefore be covered with a cloth, and kept moderately warm. A pellicle will be formed on the surface, beneath which the vinegar acquires strength: it must be kept standing for a month or two, and then put into a cask. The bunghole should be left open, and the vinegar will soon be fit for use. The prunings of the vine, being bruised and put into a vat or mash tub, and boiling water poured on them, will produce a liquor of a fine vinous quality, which may be used as vinegar.—Another method. To every pound of coarse sugar add a gallon of water; boil the mixture, and take off the scum as long as any rises. Then pour it into proper vessels, and when sufficiently cooled put into it a warm toast covered with yeast. Let it work about twenty-four hours, and then put it into an iron-bound cask, fixed either near a constant fire, or where the summer sun shines the greater part of the day. In this situation it should not be closely stopped up, but a tile or something similar should be laid on the bunghole, to keep out the dust and insects. At the end of three months or less it will be clear, and fit for use, and may be bottled off. The longer it is kept after it is bottled, the better it will be. If the vessel containing the liquor is to be exposed to the sun's heat, the best time to begin making it is in the month of April.

VINEGAR FOR SALADS. Take three ounces each of tarragon, savory, chives, and shalots, and a handful of the tops of mint and balm, all dry and pounded. Put the mixture into a wide-mouthed bottle, with a gallon of the best vinegar. Cork it down close, set it in the sun, and in a fortnight strain off and squeeze the herbs. Let it stand a day to settle, and filter it through a tammis bag.

VINEGAR WHEY. Set upon the fire as much milk as is wanted for the occasion, and when it is ready to boil, put in vinegar sufficient to turn it to a clear whey. Let it stand some minutes, and then pour it off. If too acid, a little warm water may be added. This whey is well adapted to promote perspiration. Lemon or Seville orange juice may be used instead of vinegar.

VINGARET. Chop some mint, parsley, and shalot; and mix them up with oil and vinegar. Serve the sauce in a boat, for cold fowl or meat.

VIPERS. The bites of such reptiles should constantly be guarded against as much as possible, as they are not unfrequently attended with dangerous consequences. Animals of the neat-cattle kind are more liable to be bitten and stung by these reptiles, than those of any other sort of live stock. Instances have been known where the tongues of such cattle have been even bitten or stung while grazing or feeding, which have proved fatal. Such stock are, however, seldom attacked by reptiles of the adder kind, except in cases where these are disturbed by the animals in pasturing or feeding; which is the main reason why so many of them are bitten and stung about the head, and occasionally the feet. There are mostly much pain, inflammation, and swelling produced by these bites and stings; the progress of which may commonly be checked or stopped, and the complaint removed, by the use of such means as are directed below. A sort of soft liquid of the liniment kind may be prepared by mixing strong spirit of hartshorn, saponaceous liniment, spirit of turpentine, and tincture of opium, with olive oil; the former in the proportion of about two ounces each to three of the last, incorporating them well together by shaking them in a phial, which will be found very useful in many cases. A proper quantity of it should be well rubbed upon the affected part, two or three times in the course of the day, until the inflammation and swelling begin to disappear, after the bottle has been well shaken. In the more dangerous cases, it may often be advantageous to use fomentations to the affected parts, especially when about the head, with the above application; such as those made by boiling white poppy-heads with the roots of the marshmallow, the leaves of the large plantain, and the tops of wormwood, in the quantities of a few ounces of the first, and a handful of each of the latter, when cut small, and bruised in five or six quarts of the stale grounds of malt liquor. They may be applied frequently to the diseased parts, rubbing them afterwards each time well with the above soft liquid liniment. Where there are feverish appearances, as is often the case in the summer season, a proper quantity of blood may sometimes be taken away with great benefit, and a strong purge be afterwards given of the cooling kind with much use. In slight cases of this kind, some think the continued free use of spirit of hartshorn, given internally, and applied externally to the affected parts, is the best remedy of any that is yet known. As they are so dangerous, these reptiles should always be destroyed as much as possible in all pastures and grazing grounds.

UDDER SWEET PIE. Either parboil or roast a tongue and udder, slice them into tolerably thin slices, and season them with pepper and salt. Stone half a pound of sun raisins, raise a crust, or put a puff crust round the edge of a dish, place a layer of tongue and udder at the bottom, and then some raisins, and so on till the dish is full. Cover the top with a crust, and when the pie is baked, pour in the following sauce. Beat up some yolks of eggs, with vinegar, white wine, sugar, and butter. Shake them over the fire till ready to boil, and add it to the pie immediately before it is sent to table.

ULCERS. Ulcers should not be healed precipitately, for it may be attended with considerable danger. The first object is to cleanse the wound with emollient poultices, and soften it with yellow basilicon ointment, to which may be added a little turpentine or red precipitate. They may also be washed with lime water, dressed with lint dipped in tincture of myrrh, with spermaceti, or any other cooling ointment.

UMBRELLA VARNISH. Make for umbrellas the following varnish, which will render them proof against wind and rain. Boil together two pounds of turpentine, one pound of litharge in powder, and two or three pints of linseed oil. The umbrella is then to be brushed over with the varnish, and dried in the sun.

UNIVERSAL CEMENT. To an ounce of gum mastic add as much highly rectified spirits of wine as will dissolve it. Soak an ounce of isinglass in water until quite soft, then dissolve it in pure rum or brandy, until it forms a strong glue, to which add about a quarter of an ounce of gum ammoniac well rubbed and mixed. Put the two mixtures in an earthen vessel over a gentle heat; when well united, the mixture may be put into a phial, and kept well stopped. When wanted for use, the bottle must be set in warm water, and the china or glass articles having been also warmed, the cement must be applied. It will be proper that the broken surfaces, when carefully fitted, should be kept in close contact for twelve hours at least, until the cement is fully set, after which the fracture will be found as secure as any other part of the vessel, and scarcely perceptible.

WAFERS. Dry some flour well, mix with it a little pounded sugar, and finely pounded mace. Make these ingredients into a thick batter with cream. Butter the wafer irons, and make them hot; put a tea-spoonful of the batter into them, bake them carefully, and roll them off the iron with a stick.

WAINSCOTS. Dirty painted wainscots may be cleaned with a sponge wetted in potato water, and dipped in a little fine sand. For this purpose grate some raw potatoes into water, run the pulp through a sieve, and let it stand to settle; the clear liquor will then be fit for use. If applied in a pure state, without the sand, it will be serviceable in cleaning oil paintings, and similar articles of furniture. When an oak wainscot becomes greasy, and has not been painted, it should be washed with warm beer. Then boil two quarts of ale, and put into it a piece of bees' wax the size of a walnut, with a large spoonful of sugar. Wet the wainscot all over with a brush dipped in the mixture, and when dry, rub it bright: this will give it a fine gloss.

WALNUT KETCHUP. To make the finest sort of walnut ketchup, boil or simmer a gallon of the expressed juice of walnuts when they are tender, and skim it well. Then put in two pounds of anchovies, bones and liquor; two pounds of shalot, one ounce of mace, one ounce of cloves, one of whole pepper, and one of garlic. Let all simmer together till the shalots sink; then put the liquor into a pan till cold; bottle it up, and make an equal distribution of the spice. Cork it well, and tie a bladder over. It will keep twenty years, but is not good at first. Be careful to express the juice at home, for what is sold as walnut ketchup is generally adulterated. Some people make liquor of the outside shell when the nut is ripe, but neither the colour nor the flavour is then so fine.—Another way. Take four quarts of walnut juice, two quarts of white wine vinegar, three ounces of ginger sliced, two ounces of black pepper bruised, two ounces of white pepper bruised, half a pound of anchovies; let these simmer gently, till half the quantity is evaporated; then add to it a quart of red wine, two heads of garlic, the yellow rind of eight Seville oranges, or half a pound of dried orange peel cut very small, and forty bay leaves: give it one boil together, then cover it close in an earthen vessel, and let it stand till it is cold. When it is cold put it into wide-mouthed quart bottles; and into each of the bottles put one ounce of shalots skinned and sliced: cork the bottles close, and put them by for two months, when it will be fit for use. The shalots will likewise eat very fine when taken out, though they will look of a bad colour. —Another way, for fish sauce. Take walnuts, when they are fit for pickling, bruise them well in a marble mortar, and strain off the liquor from them through a cloth, let it stand to settle, pour off the clear, and to every pint of it add one pound of anchovies, half a quarter of an ounce of mace, half a quarter of an ounce of cloves, half a quarter of an ounce of Jamaica pepper, bruised fine; boil them together till the anchovies are dissolved; then strain it off, and to the strained liquor add half a pint of the best vinegar, and eight shalots; just boil it up again, pour it into a stone pan or china bowl, and let it stand till cold, when it is fit to put up in bottles for use. It will keep for years, and is excellent with fish sauce.

WARTS AND CORNS. Warts may safely be destroyed by tying them closely round the bottom with a silk thread, or a strong flaxen thread well waxed. Or they may be dried away by some moderately corroding application, such as the milky juice of fig leaves, of swallow wort, or of spurge. Warts may also be destroyed by rubbing them with the inside of bean shells. But these corrosives can only be procured in summer; and persons who have very delicate thin skins should not use them, as they may occasion a painful swelling. Instead therefore of these applications, it may be proper to use a little vinegar impregnated with as much salt as it will dissolve. A plaster may also be made of sal ammoniac and some galbanum, which well kneaded together and applied, seldom fails of destroying them. The general and principal cause of corns is, shoes too hard and stiff, or else too small. The cure consists in softening the corns by repeated washing, and soaking the feet in warm or hot water; then cutting the corn very carefully when softened, with a sharp penknife without wounding the quick, and afterwards applying a leaf of houseleek, ground ivy, or purslain, dipped in vinegar. Or instead of these leaves, they may be dressed every day with a plaster of simple diachylon, or of gum ammoniacum softened in vinegar. The bark of the willow tree burnt to ashes, and mixed with strong vinegar, forms a lixivium which by repeated applications eradicates, warts, corns, and other cutaneous excrescences. It is however the wisest way to obviate the cause which produces them.

WASH. An infusion of horseradish in milk, makes one of the safest and best washes for the skin; or the fresh juice of houseleek, mixed with an equal quantity of new milk or cream. Honey water made rather thick, so as to form a kind of varnish on the skin, is a useful application in frosty weather, when the skin is liable to be chipped; and if it occasions any irritation or uneasiness, a little fine flour or pure hair powder should be dusted on the hands or face. A more elegant wash may be made of four ounces of potash, four ounces of rose water, and two of lemon juice, mixed in two quarts of water. A spoonful or two of this mixture put into the basin, will scent and soften the water intended to be used.

WASH BALLS. Shave thin two pounds of new white soap, into about a teacupful of rose water, and pour on as much boiling water as will soften it. Put into a brass pan a pint of sweet oil, four pennyworth of oil of almonds, half a pound of spermaceti, and dissolve the whole over the fire. Then add the soap, and half an ounce of camphor that has first been reduced to powder by rubbing it in a mortar with a few drops of spirits of wine, or lavender water, or any other scent. Boil it ten minutes, then pour it into a basin, and stir till it is quite thick enough to roll up into hard balls, which must then be done as soon as possible. If essence is used, stir it in quick after it is taken off the fire, that the scent may not fly off.

WASHING. Soda, by softening the water, saves a great deal of soap. It should be melted in a large jug of water, and some of it poured into the tubs and boiler; and when the lather becomes weak, more is to be added. The new improvement in soft soap is, if properly used, a saving of nearly half in quantity; and though something dearer than the hard, it reduces the expence of washing considerably. Many good laundresses advise soaping linen in warm water the night previous to washing, as facilitating the operation with less friction.

WASPS. These insects are not only destructive to grapes, peaches, and the more delicate kinds of fruit, but also to bees; the hives of which they attack and plunder, frequently compelling those industrious inmates to forsake their habitation. About the time when the wasps begin to appear, several phials should be filled three parts full of a mixture consisting of the lees of beer or wine, and the sweepings of sugar, or the dregs of molasses, and suspended by yellow packthread on nails in the garden wall. When the bottles are filled with insects, the liquor must be poured into another vial, and the wasps crushed on the ground. If they settle on wall fruit, they may be destroyed by touching them with a feather dipped in oil; or may be taken with birdlime put on the end of a stick or lath, and touched while sitting on the fruit. The number of these noxious insects might be greatly reduced by searching for their nests in the spring of the year. The places to find them are at new posts, pales, melon frames, or any solid timber; for as they make their combs of the shavings of sound wood, which they rasp off with their fangs, and moisten up with a mucus from their bodies, they may often be found near such materials.

WATER. As it is difficult in some places to obtain a sufficient quantity of fresh spring water for constant use, especially in large towns and cities, it is important to know that river water or such as becomes turbid, may be rendered fit for use by the following easy experiment. Dissolve half an ounce of alum in a pint of warm water, and stir it about in a puncheon of water taken from the river; the impurities will soon settle to the bottom, and in a day or two it will become as clear as the finest spring water. To purify any kind of water that has become foul by being stagnant, place a piece of wicker work in the middle of a vessel; spread on this a layer of charcoal four or five inches thick, and above the charcoal a quantity of sand. The surface of the sand is to be covered with paper pierced full of holes, to prevent the water from making channels in the sand. The water to be purified is to be poured on, to filter through the sand and charcoal, and the filter is to be removed occasionally. By this simple process, any person may procure good limpid water at a very trifling expense, and preserve what would otherwise become useless and offensive.

WATER FOR BREWING. The most proper water for brewing is soft river water, which has had the rays of the sun, and the influence of the air upon it, which have a tendency to permit it easily to penetrate the malt, and extract its virtues. On the contrary, hard waters astringe and bind the power of the malt, so that its virtues are not freely communicated to the liquor. Some people hold it as a maxim, that all water that will mix with soap is fit for brewing, which is the case with the generality of river water; and it has frequently been found from experience, that when an equal quantity of malt has been used to a barrel of river water, as to a barrel of spring water, the brewing from the former has exceeded the other in strength above five degrees in the course of twelve months keeping. It has also been observed, that the malt was not only the same in quantity for one barrel as for the other, but was the same in quality, having all been measured from the same heap. The hops were also the same, both in quality and in quantity, and the time of boiling equal in each. They were worked in the same manner, and tunned and kept in the same cellar; a proof that the water only could be the cause of the difference. Dorchester beer, which is generally in much esteem, is chiefly brewed with chalky water, which is plentiful in almost every part of that county; and as the soil is mostly chalk, the cellars, being dug in that dry soil, contribute much to the good keeping of their drink, it being of a close texture, and of a dry quality, so as to dissipate damps; for it has been found by experience, that damp cellars are equally injurious to the casks and the good keeping of the liquor. Where water is naturally of a hard quality, it may in some measure be softened by an exposure to the sun and air, and by infusing in it some pieces of soft chalk; or when the water is set on to boil, in order to be poured on the malt, put into it a quantity of bran, and it will have a very good effect.

WATER CAKES. Dry three pounds of fine flour, and rub into it a pound of sifted sugar, a pound of butter, and an ounce of carraway seeds. Make it into a paste with three quarters of a pint of boiling new milk; roll the paste very thin, and cut it into any form or size. Punch the cakes full of holes, and bake on tin plates in a cool oven.

WATER GRUEL. Mix by degrees a large spoonful of oatmeal with a pint of water in a saucepan, and when smooth, boil it. Or rub the oatmeal smooth in a little water, and put it into a pint of water boiling on the fire. Stir it well, and boil it quick, but do not suffer it to boil over. In a quarter of an hour strain it off, add salt and a bit of butter when eaten, and stir it together till the whole is incorporated. To make it however in the quickest manner, mix a spoonful of ground oatmeal very smooth, with as much hot water as will just liquify it. Then gradually pour upon it a pint of boiling water, stirring it all the time to keep it smooth. It may be cooled by pouring it from one basin to another till it is fit to drink. Water gruel made in this way is very smooth and good, and being prepared in a few minutes, it is particularly useful when wanted in haste, to assist the operation of medicine.

WATER PIPES. To prevent their freezing when full of water, preserve a little circulation by leaving the cock dripping; or by tying up the ball cock during the winter's frost, the water may be preserved for use. Care should be taken however to lay the pipe which supplies the cistern in such a position as not to retain the water, and of course it will not be liable to freeze.

WATER SOUCHY. Stew two or three flounders, some parsley leaves and roots, thirty peppercorns, and a quart of water, till the fish are boiled to pieces, and then pulp them through a sieve. Set over the fire the pulped fish, the liquor that boiled them, some perch, tench, and flounders, and some fresh leaves or roots of parsley. Simmer them together till done enough, and serve in a deep dish. Slices of bread and butter are to be sent to table, to eat with the souchy.

WAX. Bees' wax is obtained from the combs, after the sweet and liquid parts are extracted, by heating and pressing them between iron plates. The best sort is firm and hard, of a clear yellow colour and an agreeable odour, similar to that of honey. New wax is tough, yet easily broken; by long keeping it becomes harder and more brittle, loses its colour, and partly also its fragrance. With a view to bleach the wax, it is cut into small pieces, melted, and poured into cold water. In this state it is exposed to the sun, afterwards melted again, poured into water, and exposed to the air, two or three times over, till it is perfectly blanched. It is then dissolved for the last time, cast into flat moulds, and again exposed to the air for a day or two, in order to render it more transparent.

WAX PLASTER. This is made of a pound of yellow wax, half a pound of white rosin, and three quarters of mutton suet, melted together. This forms a proper plaster for blisters, and in other cases where a gentle digestive is necessary.

WEAK EYES. Dimness of sight, arising from weakness or inflammation, is best relieved by frequent washing of the eyes with cold water. If this do not succeed, the following solution may be applied. Dissolve four grains each of the sugar of lead and crude sal-ammoniac, in eight ounces of water, to which a few drops of laudanum may occasionally be added, and bathe the eyes with it night and morning. A tea-spoonful of brandy in a cup of water will also make good eye-water, or a little simple rose water may supply the place.

WEDDING CAKE. Take two pounds of butter, beat it to a cream with the hand, and put in two pounds of fine sugar sifted. Mix well together two pounds of fine dried flour, half a pound of almonds blanched and pounded with orange-flower water, and an ounce of beaten mace. Beat up sixteen eggs, leaving out three whites, and put to them half a glass of sack, and the same of brandy. Put a handful of the flour and almonds to the sugar and butter, then a spoonful of the eggs, and so on till they are all mixed together. Beat it an hour with the hand, add two pounds of currants, half a pound of citron, half a pound of orange peel, and two spoonfuls of orange-flower water. Butter the tin, and bake it three hours and a half. An iceing should be put over the cake after it is baked.

WEEDS. Weeds are in their most succulent state in the month of June, and there is scarcely a hedge border but might be rendered useful by mowing them at this season, but which afterwards would become a nuisance. After the weeds have lain a few hours to wither, hungry cattle will eat them with great freedom, and it would display the appearance of good management to embrace the transient opportunity.

WELCH ALE. To brew very fine Welch ale, pour forty-two gallons of hot but not boiling water, on eight bushels of malt; cover it up, and let it stand three hours. Mean while infuse four pounds of hops in a little hot water, and put the water and hops into a tub; run the wort upon them, and boil them together three hours. Strain off the hops, and reserve them for the small beer. Let the wort stand in a high tub till cool enough to receive the yeast, of which put in two quarts of the best quality: mix it thoroughly and often. When the wort has done working, the second or third day, the yeast will sink rather than rise in the middle: remove it then, and tun the ale as it works out. Pour in a quart at a time gently, to prevent the fermentation from continuing too long, which weakens the liquor. Put paper over the bung-hole two or three days before it is closed up.

WELCH BEEF. Rub three ounces of saltpetre into a good piece of the round or buttock. After four hours apply a handful of common salt, a quarter of an ounce of Jamaica pepper, and the same of black pepper, mixed together. Continue it in the pickle a fortnight, then stuff it with herbs, cover it with a thick paste, and bake it. Take off the paste, pour the liquor from it, and pour over it some melted beef suet.

WELCH PUDDING. Melt half a pound of fine butter gently, beat with it the yolks of eight and the whites of four eggs. Mix in six ounces of loaf sugar, and the rind of a lemon grated. Put a paste into a dish for turning out, pour in the batter, and bake it nicely.

WELCH RABBIT. Toast a slice of bread on both sides, and butter it. Toast a slice of Gloucester cheese on one side, and lay that on the bread; then toast the other side with a salamander, rub mustard over, and serve it up hot under a cover.

WENS. These are prevalent chiefly among the inhabitants of marshy countries, bordering on rivers and standing waters, especially among females, and persons of a delicate habit; but they very often arise from scrophula. Camphor mixed with sweet oil, or a solution of sal ammoniac, have often been applied to these tumours with success. In Derbyshire, where this disorder greatly prevails, they use the following preparation. Fifteen grains of burnt sponge are beaten up with a similar quantity of millipede, and from eight to ten grains of cinnabar antimony. The whole is to be mixed with honey, and taken every morning before breakfast.

WESTPHALIA HAM. Rub the ham with half a pound of coarse sugar, let it lie twelve hours, then rub it with an ounce of saltpetre pounded, and a pound of common salt. Let it lie three weeks, turning it every day. Dry it over a wood fire, and put a pint of oak sawdust into the water when it is boiled.—Another way. Take spring water that is not hard, add saltpetre and bay salt to it till it will bear an egg, the broad way, then add a pound and a half of coarse sugar; mix all together, and let the ham lay in this pickle a fortnight or three weeks; then lay it in the chimney to dry. When you boil it, put some hay into the copper with it. You may keep the pickle as long as you please by often boiling it up.

WET CLOTHES. When a person has the misfortune to get wet, care should be taken not to get too near the fire, or into a warm room, so as to occasion a sudden heat. The safest way is to keep in constant motion, until some dry clothes can be procured, and to exchange them as soon as possible.

WHEAT BREAD. To make it in the most economical way, the coarsest of the bran only is to be taken from the flour, and the second coat, or what is called pollard, is to be left in the meal. Five pounds of the bran are to be boiled in somewhat more than four gallons of water, in order that, when perfectly smooth, three gallons and three quarts of clear bran water may be poured into and kneaded up with forty-six pounds of the meal; adding salt as well as yeast, in the same way as for other bread. When the dough is ready to bake, the loaves are to be made up, and baked two hours and a half in a tolerably hot oven. As flour when thus made up will imbibe three quarts more of this bran liquor than of common water, it evidently produces not only a more nutricious and substantial food, but increases one fifth above the usual quantity; consequently it makes a saving of at least one day's consumption in every week. If this meal bread were in general use, it would be a saving to the nation of nearly ten millions a year. Besides, this bread has the following peculiar property: if put into the oven and baked for twenty minutes, after it is ten days old, it will appear again like new bread.

WHEAT EARS. To roast wheat ears and ortolans, they should be spitted sideways, with a vine leaf between each. Baste them with butter, and strew them with bread crumbs while roasting. Ten or twelve minutes will do them. Serve them up with fried bread crumbs in the dish, and gravy in a tureen.

WHEY. Cheese whey is a very wholesome drink for weakly persons, especially when the cows are in fresh pasture. Tending to quench thirst, and to promote sleep, it is well adapted to feverish constitutions. It is the most relaxing and diluting of all drinks, dissolving and carrying off the salts, and is a powerful remedy in the hot scurvy.

WHEY BUTTER. The whey is first set in mugs, to acquire a sufficient degree of consistence and sourness for churning, either by the warmth of the season, or by a fire, as in the making of milk butter. Sometimes the green and white whey are boiled together, and turned by a little sour ale. When the green whey is boiled alone, it is necessary to keep it over the fire about half an hour, till it begins to break and separate, but it must be allowed to simmer only. The process is much the same as in milk butter, but it will keep only a few days, and does not cut so firm as the butter which is made of cream.

WHIGS. Mix with two pounds of fine flour, half a pound of sugar pounded and sifted, and an ounce of carraway seeds. Melt half a pound of butter in a pint of milk; when as warm as new milk, put to it three eggs, leaving out one white, and a spoonful of yeast. Mix them well together, and let the paste stand four hours to rise. Make them into whigs, and bake them on buttered tins.—Another way. Rub half a pound of butter into a pound and a half of flour, add a quarter of a pound of sugar, a very little salt, and three spoonfuls of new yeast. Make it into a light paste with warm milk, let it stand an hour to rise, and then form it into whigs. Bake them upon sheets of tin in a quick oven. Carraway seeds may be added if preferred.—Another way. Take two pounds and a half of flour, dry it before the fire, and when cold rub in a quarter of a pound of fresh butter, and six ounces of sugar; mix half a pint of yeast that is not bitter, with warm milk, put this to the flour with some carraway seeds; mix all together to a light dough, set it before the fire to rise, then make it into what shape you please; bake them in a slack oven. You may add allspice beat fine, instead of carraways, if you please.—Another way. Take a pound and a half of flour, add a quarter of a pint of ale yeast to half a pint of warm milk, mix these together, and let it lie by the fire half an hour; then work in half a pound of sugar and half a pound of fresh butter to a paste; make them up, and let them be put into a quick oven.

WHIPT CREAM. Take a quart of thick cream, the whites of eight eggs well beaten, with half a pint of sack; mix all together, and sweeten it to your taste, with double-refined sugar; (you may perfume it if you please, with a little musk, or ambergris, tied in a piece of muslin, and steeped a little while in the cream) pare a lemon, and tie some of the peel in the middle of the whisk, then whip up the cream, take off the froth with a spoon, and lay it in the glasses, or basons. This does well over a fine tart.

WHIPT SYLLABUBS. Put some rich cream into an earthen pot, add some white wine, lemon juice, and sugar to the taste. Mill them well together with a chocolate mill, and as the froth keeps rising take it off with a spoon, and put it into syllabub glasses. They should be made the day before they are to be used. Syllabubs are very pretty in the summer time made with red currant juice, instead of lemon juice.—Another way. Take a quart of cream, boil it, and let it stand till cold; then take a pint of white wine, pare a lemon thin, and steep the peel in the wine two hours before you use it; to this add the juice of a lemon, and as much sugar as will make it very sweet; put all together into a bowl, and whisk it one way till it is pretty thick, fill the glasses, and keep it a day before you use it. It will keep good for three or four days. Let the cream be full measure, and the wine rather less; if you like it perfumed, put in a grain or two of ambergris.—Another way. To a quart of thick cream put half a pint of sack, the juice of two Seville oranges, or lemons, grate the peel of two lemons, and add half a pound of double-refined sugar well pounded; mix a little sack with sugar, and put it into some of the glasses, and red wine and sugar into others, the rest fill with syllabub only. Then whisk your cream up very well, take off the froth with a spoon, and fill the glasses carefully, as full as they will hold. Observe, that this sort must not be made long before they are used.

WHITE BREAD. This is made the same as household bread, except that it consists of fine flour unmixed. The water to be used should be lukewarm in summer, and in very cold weather it must be hot, but not so as to scald the yeast. Bricks are made by moulding the loaves long instead of round, and cutting the sides in several places before they are put into the oven.

WHITE CAKES. Dry half a pound of flour, rub into it a very little pounded sugar, one ounce of butter, an egg, a few carraways, and as much milk and water as will make it into a paste. Roll it thin, cut it into little cakes with a wine glass, or the top of a canister, and bake them fifteen minutes on tin plates.

WHITE CAUDLE. Boil four spoonfuls of oatmeal in two quarts of water, with a blade or two of mace, and a piece of lemon peel; stir it often, and let it boil a full quarter of an hour, then strain it through a sieve for use; when you use it, grate in some nutmeg, sweeten it to your palate, and add what white wine you think proper: if it is not for a sick person, you may squeeze in a little lemon juice.

WHITE CERATE. Take four ounces of olive oil, half an ounce of spermaceti, and four ounces of white wax. Put them into an earthen pipkin, and stir the mixture with a stick till it is quite cold.

WHITE GRAVY. Boil in a quart of water a pound and a half of veal, from the knuckle or scrag end of the neck. Add a small onion, a bunch of sweet herbs, a blade of mace, a little whole pepper and salt. After an hour's simmering over the fire, strain off the gravy, and it is ready for use.

WHITE GRAVY FOR SOUPS. To a few slices of lean ham, add a knuckle of veal cut in pieces, some turnips, parsnips, leeks, onions, and celery. Put them all into a stewpan with two quarts of water, and let it simmer till the meat is nearly tender, without allowing it to colour. Add to this half as much clear beef gravy, and boil it an hour, skimming off the fat very clean. Strain it, and set it by for use.

WHITE HERRINGS. If good, their gills are of a fine red, and the eyes bright; as is likewise the whole fish, which must be stiff and firm. Having scaled, drawn, and cleaned them, dust them with flour, and fry them of a light brown. Plain or melted butter for sauce.

WHITE LEAD. White oxide of lead is often adulterated by the carbonate of lime. To detect this pour four drams of pure acetous acid, over a dram of the suspected oxide. This will dissolve both oxide and chalk; but if a few drops of a solution of oxalic acid be now poured in, a very abundant white precipitate of oxalate of lime will take place.

WHITE PAINT. An excellent substitute for white oil paint may be made of fresh curds bruised fine, and kneaded with an equal quantity of slacked lime. The mixture is to be well stirred, without any water, and it will produce an excellent white paint for inside work. As it dries very quickly, it should be used as soon as made; and if two coats be laid on, it may afterwards be polished with a woollen cloth till it becomes as bright as varnish. If applied to places exposed to moisture, the painting should be rubbed over with the yolk of an egg, which will render it as durable as the best of oil painting. No kind of painting can be so cheap; and as it dries speedily, two coats of it may be laid on in a day and polished, and no offensive smell will arise from it.

WHITE POT. The antient way of making a white pot is to put the yolks of four or five eggs well beaten to a pint of cream, adding some pulps of apples, sugar, spices, and sippets of white bread. It may be baked either in a dish, or in a crust.—Another way. Beat eight eggs, leaving out four whites, with a little rose water; strain them to two quarts of new milk, and a small nutmeg grated, and sugar to your taste; cut a French roll in thin slices, and lay in the bottom of a soup dish (after buttering it) then pour over your milk and eggs, and bake it in a slow oven.

WHITE PUDDINGS. Pour two pints and a half of scalding hot milk upon half a pound of Naples biscuits, or bread; let it stand uncovered, and when well soaked, bruise the bread very fine. Add half a pound of almonds well beaten with orange-flower water, three quarters of a pound of sugar, a pound of beef suet or marrow shred fine, a quarter of an ounce of salt, ten yolks of eggs and five whites. Mix the whole thoroughly together, and put it into the skins well prepared, filling them but half full, and tying them at proper distances like sausages. The skins must be carefully cleaned, and laid in rose water some hours before they are used. Currants may be used instead of almonds, if preferred.

WHITE HOG'S PUDDINGS. When the skins have been well soaked and cleaned, rinse and soak them all night in rose water, and put into them the following preparation. Mix half a pound of blanched almonds cut into seven or eight parts, with a pound of grated bread, two pounds of marrow or rich suet, a pound of currants, some beaten cinnamon, cloves, mace, and nutmeg; a quart of cream, the yolks of six and whites of two eggs, a little orange-flower water, a little fine Lisbon sugar, and some lemon peel and citron sliced, and half fill the skins. To know whether it be sweet enough, warm a little in a panikin. Much care must be taken in boiling, to prevent the puddings from bursting. Prick them with a small fork as they rise, and boil them in milk and water. Lay them in a table cloth till cold.

WHITE ONION SAUCE. Peel half a dozen white Spanish onions, cut them in half, and lay them in a pan of spring water for a quarter of an hour. Boil them an hour, or till quite tender, drain them well on a hair sieve, and then chop and bruise them fine. Put them into a clean saucepan with flour and butter, half a tea-spoonful of salt, and some cream or good milk. Stir it till it boils, rub the whole through a sieve, adding milk or cream to make it of a proper thickness. This is the usual sauce for boiled rabbits, mutton, or tripe; but there requires plenty of it.

WHITE SAUCE. This favourite sauce is equally adapted to fowls, fricassee, rabbits, white meat, fish, and vegetables; and it is seldom necessary to purchase any fresh meat to make it, as the proportion of that flavour is but small. The liquor in which fowls, veal, or rabbit have been boiled, will answer the purpose; or the broth of whatever meat happens to be in the house, such as necks of chickens, raw or dressed veal. Stew with a little water any of these, with a bit of lemon peel, some sliced onion, some white peppercorns, a little pounded mace or nutmeg, and a bunch of sweet herbs. Keep it on the fire till the flavour is good; then strain it, and add a little good cream, a piece of butter, a very little flour, and salt to your taste. A squeeze of lemon may be added after the sauce is taken off the fire, shaking it well. Yolk of egg is often used in fricassee, cream is better, as the former is apt to curdle.

WHITE SOUP. Take a scrag of mutton, a knuckle of veal, after cutting off as much meat as will make collops, two or three shank bones of mutton nicely cleaned, and a quarter of very fine undressed lean gammon of bacon. Add a bunch of sweet herbs, a piece of fresh lemon peel, two or three onions, three blades of mace, and a dessert-spoonful of white pepper. Boil all in three quarts of water, till the meat falls quite to pieces. Next day take off the fat, clear the jelly from the sediment, and put it into a nice tin saucepan. If maccaroni be used, it should be added soon enough to get perfectly tender, after soaking in cold water. Vermicelli may be added after the thickening, as it requires less time to do. Prepare the thickening beforehand thus: blanch a quarter of a pound of sweet almonds, and beat them to a paste in a marble mortar, with a spoonful of water to prevent their oiling. Then mince a large slice of cold veal or chicken, and beat it with a piece of stale white bread; add all this to a pint of thick cream, a bit of fresh lemon peel, and a blade of pounded mace. Boil it a few minutes, add to it a pint of soup, and strain and pulp it through a coarse sieve. This thickening is then fit for putting to the rest, which should boil for half an hour afterwards.—To make a plainer white soup, boil a small knuckle of veal, till the liquor is reduced to three pints. Add seasoning as above, and a quarter of a pint of good milk. Two spoonfuls of cream, and a little ground rice, will give it a proper thickness. The meat and the soup may both be served together.—Another. Take a scrag or knuckle of veal, slices of undressed gammon of bacon, onions, mace, and simmer them in a small quantity of water, till it is very strong. Lower it with a good beef broth made the day before, and stew it till the meat is done to rags. Add cream, vermicelli, a roll, and almonds.

WHITE WINE WHEY. Set on the fire half a pint of new milk; the moment it boils up, pour in as much sound raisin wine as will completely turn it, and until it looks clear. Let it boil up, then set the saucepan aside till the curd subsides, and do not stir it. Pour the whey off, add to it half a pint of boiling water, and a little lump sugar. The whey will thus be cleared of milky particles, and may be made to any degree of weakness.

WHITINGS. These may be had almost at any time, but are chiefly in season during the first three months of the year. In choosing them, the firmness of the body and fins is chiefly to be looked to; and in places where there is no regular supply of fish, it will be found an accommodation to dry them for keeping. The largest are best for this purpose. Take out the gills, the eyes, and the entrails, and remove the blood from the backbone. Wipe them dry, salt the inside, and lay them on a board for the night. Hang them up in a dry place, and after three or four days they will be fit to eat. When to be dressed, skin and rub them over with egg, and cover them with bread crumbs. Lay them before the fire, baste with butter till sufficiently browned, and serve them with egg sauce.

WHITLOWS. As soon as the disorder is apparent, the finger affected is to be plunged into warm water, or the steam of boiling water may be applied to it. The application must be very frequently repeated the first day, and the complaint will soon be dispersed. Unfortunately however it is too generally supposed, that such slight attacks can have only slight consequences, and hence they are too apt to be neglected till the complaint has considerably increased. But in this state no time should be lost in resorting to skilful advice, as the danger attending these small tumours is much greater than is usually imagined.

WHOLE RICE PANCAKES. Stew half a pound of whole rice in water till it is very tender, and let it stand in a basin to cool. Break it small, put to it half a pint of scalded cream, half a pound of clarified butter, a handful of flour, a little nutmeg and salt, and five eggs well beaten. Stir these well together, and fry them in butter or lard. Serve them up with sugar sifted over them, and a Seville orange or lemon cut and laid round the dish. This preparation may be made into a pudding, either baked or boiled, and with currants added or not, as approved. Three quarters of an hour will bake it, and an hour will boil it.

WHOLE RICE PUDDING. Stew very gently a quarter of a pound of whole rice, in a pint and a half of new milk. When the rice is tender, pour it into a basin, stir in a piece of butter, and let it stand till quite cool. Then put in four eggs, a little salt, some nutmeg and sugar. Boil it an hour in a basin well buttered.

WILD DUCKS. A wild duck, or a widgeon, will require twenty or twenty-five minutes roasting, according to the size. A teal, from fifteen to twenty minutes; and other birds of this kind, in proportion to their size, a longer or a shorter time. Baste them with butter, and take them up with the gravy in, sprinkling a little over them before they are quite done. Serve them up with shalot sauce in a boat, or with good gravy, and lemons cut in quarters.

WILD FOWL. Season with salt and pepper, and put a piece of butter into each; but the flavour is best preserved without stuffing. To take off the fishy taste which wild fowl sometimes have, put an onion, salt, and hot water, into the dripping pan, and baste them with this for the first ten minutes: then take away the pan, and baste constantly with butter. Wild fowl require much less dressing than tame: they should be served of a fine colour, and well frothed up. A rich brown gravy should be sent in the dish; and when the breast is cut into slices, before taking off the bone, a squeeze of lemon, with pepper and salt, is a great improvement to the flavour.

WILTSHIRE BACON. The way to cure Wiltshire bacon is to sprinkle the flitch with salt, and let the blood drain off for twenty-four hours. Then mix a pound and a half of coarse sugar, the same quantity of bay salt, not quite so much as half a pound of saltpetre, and a pound of common salt. Rub this mixture well on the bacon, turning it every day for a month: then hang it to dry, and afterwards smoke it ten days. The quantity of salts above mentioned is sufficient for the whole hog.

WILTSHIRE CHEESE. This is made of new milk, a little lowered with water and skim milk. The curd is first broken with the hand and dish, care being taken to let the whey run off gradually, to prevent its carrying away with it the fat of the cowl. For thin cheese the curd is not broken so fine as in Gloucestershire; for thick cheese it is crushed finer still. The whey is poured off as it rises, and the curd pressed down. The mass is then pared down three or four times over, in slices about an inch thick, in order to extract all the whey from it, and then it is pressed and scalded as before. After separating the whey, the curd is sometimes broken again, and salted in the cowl; and at others it is taken warm out of the liquor, and salted in the vat. Thin cheeses are placed in one layer, with a small handful of salt; and thick ones in two layers, with two handfuls of salt; the salt being spread and rubbed uniformly among the curd.

WINDSOR BEANS. These should be boiled in plenty of water, with a little salt, and be put in when the water boils. Serve them up with boiled bacon, and parsley and butter in a boat.

WINDSOR BEANS FRICASSEED. When grown large, but not mealy, boil, blanch, and lay them in a white sauce previously heated up. Warm them through in the sauce, and serve them up. No beans but what are of a fine green should be used for this dish.

WINDSOR PUDDING. Shred half a pound of suet very fine, grate into it half a pound of French roll, a little nutmeg, and the rind of a lemon. Add to these half a pound of chopped apple, half a pound of currants clean washed and fried, half a pound of jar raisins stoned and chopped, a glass of rich sweet wine, and five eggs well beaten, with a little salt. Mix all thoroughly together, and boil it in a basin or mould for three hours. Sift fine sugar over it when sent to table, and pour white wine sauce into the dish.

WINDSOR SOAP. Cut the best white soap into thin slices, melt it over a slow fire, and scent it with oil of carraway, or any other agreeable perfume. Shaving boxes may then be filled with the melted soap, or it may be poured into a small drawer or any other mould; and after it has stood a few days to dry, it may be cut into square pieces ready for use.

WINE. The moderate use of wine is highly conducive to health, especially in weak and languid habits, and in convalescents who are recovering from the attacks of malignant fevers. Hence it forms an extensive article of commerce, and immense quantities are consumed in this country. But nothing is more capable of being adulterated, or of producing more pernicious effects on the human constitution, and therefore it requires the strictest attention. A few simple means only will be sufficient to detect such adulterations, and to prevent their fatal consequences. If new white wine, for example, be of a sweetish flavour, and leave a certain astringency on the tongue; if it has an unusually high colour, disproportionate to its nominal age and real strength; or if it has a strong pungent taste, resembling that of brandy or other ardent spirits, such liquor may be considered as adulterated. When old wine presents either a very pale or a very deep colour, or possesses a very tart and astringent taste, and deposits a thick crust on the sides or bottom of glass vessels, it has then probably been coloured with some foreign substance. This may easily be detected by passing the liquor through filtering paper, when the colouring ingredients will remain on the surface. The fraud may also be discovered by filling a small vial with the suspected wine, and closing its mouth with the finger: the bottle is then to be inverted, and immersed in a basin of clear water. The finger being withdrawn, the tinging or adulterating matter will pass into the water, so that the former may be observed sinking to the bottom by its own weight. Wines becoming tart or sour, are frequently mixed with the juice of carrots and turnips; and if this do not recover the sweetness to a sufficient degree, alum or the sugar of lead is sometimes added; but which cannot fail to be productive of the worst effects, and will certainly operate as slow poison. To detect the alum, let the suspected liquor be mixed with a little lime water. At the end of ten or twelve hours the composition must be filtered, and if crystals be formed, it contains no alum. But if it be adulterated, the sediment will split into small segments, which will adhere to the filtering paper on which it is spread. In order to detect the litharge or sugar of lead, a few drops of the solution of yellow orpiment and quicklime should be poured into a glass of wine. If the colour of the liquor change, and become successively dark red, black or brown, it is an evident proof of its being adulterated with lead. As orpiment is poisonous, it would be better to use a few drops of vitriolic acid for this purpose, which should be introduced into a small quantity of the suspected liquor. This will cause the lead to sink to the bottom of the glass, in the form of a white powder. A solution of hepatic gas in distilled water, if added to wine sophisticated with lead, will produce a black sediment, and thus discover the smallest quantity of that poisonous metal; but in pure wine, no precipitation will take place.

The following preparation has been proved to be a sufficient test for adulterated wine or cider. Let one dram of the dry liver of sulphur, and two drams of the cream of tartar, be shaken in two ounces of distilled water, till the whole become saturated with hepatic gas: the mixture is then to be filtered through blotting paper, and kept in a vial closely corked. In order to try the purity of wine, about twenty drops of this test are to be poured into a small glass: if the wine only become turbid with white clouds, and a similar sediment be deposited, it is then not impregnated with any metallic ingredients. But if it turn black or muddy, its colour approach to a deep red, and its taste be at first sweet, and then astringent, the liquor certainly contains the sugar, or other pernicious preparation of lead. The presence of iron is indicated by the wine acquiring a dark blue coat, after the test is put in, similar to that of pale ink; and if there be any particles of copper or verdigris, a blackish grey sediment will be formed. A small portion of sulphur is always mixed with white wines, in order to preserve them; but if too large a quantity be employed, the wine thus impregnated becomes injurious. Sulphur however may easily be detected, for if a piece of an egg shell, or of silver, be immersed in the wine, it instantly acquires a black hue. Quicklime is also mixed with wine, for imparting a beautiful red colour. Its presence may easily be ascertained by suffering a little wine to stand in a glass for two or three days; when the lime, held in solution, will appear on the surface in the form of a thin pellicle or crust. The least hurtful but most common adulteration of wine, is that of mixing it with water, which may be detected by throwing into it a small piece of quicklime. If it slack or dissolve the lime, the wine must have been diluted; but if the contrary, which will seldom be the case, the liquor may be considered as genuine.

WINE COOLED. The best way of cooling wine or other liquors in hot weather, is to dip a cloth in cold water, and wrap it round the bottle two or three times, then place it in the sun. The process should be renewed once or twice.

WINE POSSET. Boil some slices of white bread in a quart of milk. When quite soft, take it off the fire, grate in half a nutmeg, and a little sugar. Pour it out, and add by degrees a pint of sweet wine, and serve it with toasted bread.

WINE REFINED. In order to refine either wine or cider, beat up the whites and shells of twenty eggs. Mix a quart of the liquor with them, and put it into the cask. Stir it well to the bottom, let it stand half an hour, and stop it up close. In a few days it may be bottled off.

WINE ROLL. Soak a penny French roll in raisin wine till it will hold no more: put it in a dish, and pour round it a custard, or cream, sugar, and lemon juice. Just before it is served, sprinkle over it some nonpareil comfits, or stick into it a few blanched almonds slit. Sponge biscuits may be used instead of the roll.

WINE SAUCE. For venison or hare, mix together a quarter of a pint of claret or port, the same quantity of plain mutton gravy, and a table-spoonful of currant jelly. Let it just boil up, and send it to table in a sauce boat.

WINE VINEGAR. After making raisin wine, when the fruit has been strained, lay it on a heap to heat; then to every hundred weight, put fifteen gallons of water. Set the cask in the sun, and put in a toast of yeast. As vinegar is so necessary an article in a family, and one on which so great a profit is made, a barrel or two might always be kept preparing, according to what suited. If the raisins of wine were ready, that kind might be made; if gooseberries be cheap and plentiful, then gooseberry vinegar may be preferred; or if neither, then the sugar vinegar; so that the cask need not be left empty, or be liable to grow musty.

WINE WHEY. Put on the fire a pint of milk and water, and the moment it begins to boil, pour in as much sweet wine as will turn it into whey, and make it look clear. Boil it up, and let it stand off the fire till the curd all sinks to the bottom. Do not stir it, but pour off the whey for use. Or put a pint of skimmed milk and half a pint of white wine into a basin, let it stand a few minutes, and pour over it a pint of boiling water. When the curd has settled to the bottom, pour off the whey, and put in a piece of lump sugar, a sprig of balm, or a slice of lemon.

WINTER VEGETABLES. To preserve several vegetables to eat in the winter, observe the following rules. French beans should be gathered young, and put into a little wooden keg, a layer of them about three inches deep. Then sprinkle them with salt, put another layer of beans, and so on till the keg is full, but be careful not to sprinkle too much salt. Lay over them a plate, or a cover of wood that will go into the keg, and put a heavy stone upon it. A pickle will rise from the beans and salt; and if they are too salt, the soaking and boiling will not be sufficient to make them palatable. When they are to be eaten, they must be cut, soaked, and boiled as fresh beans. Carrots, parsnips, and beet root, should be kept in layers of dry sand, and neither they nor potatoes should be cleared from the earth. Store onions keep best hung up in a dry cold room. Parsley should be cut close to the stalks, and dried in a warm room, or on tins in a very cool oven. Its flavour and colour may thus be preserved, and will be found useful in winter. Artichoke bottoms, slowly dried, should be kept in paper bags. Truffles, morels, and lemon peel, should be hung in a dry place, and ticketed. Small close cabbages, laid on a stone floor before the frost sets in, will blanch and be very fine, after many weeks' keeping.

WOOD. An excellent glue, superior to the common sort, and suitable for joining broken furniture or any kind of wood, may be made of an ounce of isinglass dissolved in a pint of brandy. The isinglass should be pounded, dissolved by gentle heat, strained through a piece of muslin, and kept in a glass closely stopped. When required for use, it should be dissolved with moderate heat, and applied the same as common glue. Its effect is so powerful as to join the parts of wood stronger than the wood itself, but should not be exposed to damp or moisture.

WOODCOCKS. These will keep good for several days. Roast them without drawing, and serve them on toast. The thigh and back are esteemed the best. Butter only should be eaten with them, as gravy diminishes the fineness of the flavour. To roast woodcocks and snipes in the French method, take out the trails and chop them, except the stomachs, with some minced bacon, or a piece of butter. Add some parsley and chives, and a little salt. Put this stuffing into the birds, sow up the opening, and roast them with bacon covered with paper. Serve them up with Spanish sauce.

WOOLLENS. To preserve articles of this sort from the moths, let them be well brushed and shaken, and laid up cool and dry. Then mix among them bitter apples from the druggists', in small muslin bags, carefully sewn up in several folds of linen, and turned in at the edges.

WORMS. A strong decoction of walnut tree leaves thrown upon the ground where there are worm casts, will cause them to rise up. They may then be given to the poultry, or thrown into the fish pond. Salt and water, or a ley of wood ashes, poured into worm-holes on a gravel walk, will effectually destroy them. Sea water, the brine of salted meat, or soot, will be found to answer the same purpose.

WORMS. Worms in children are denoted by paleness of the face, itching of the nose, grinding of the teeth during sleep, offensive breath, and nausea. The belly is hard and painful, and in the morning there is a copious flow of saliva, and an uncommon craving for dry food. Amongst a variety of other medicines for destroying worms in the human body, the following will be found effectual. Make a solution of tartarised antimony, two grains in four ounces of water, and take two or three tea-spoonfuls three times a day, for four days; and on the following day a purging powder of calomel and jalap, from three to six grains each. Or take half a pound of senna leaves well bruised, and twelve ounces of olive oil, and digest them together in a sand heat for four or five days. Strain off the liquor, take a spoonful in the morning fasting, persevere in it, and it will be found effectual in the most obstinate cases. A more simple remedy is to pour some port wine into a pewter dish, and let it stand for twenty-four hours. Half a common wine-glassful is a sufficient dose for an infant, and a whole one for an adult.

WORMWOOD ALE. The proper way to make all sorts of herb drinks, is to gather the herbs in the right season. Then dry them in the shade, and put them into closed paper bags. When they are wanted for use, take out the proper quantity, put it into a linen bag, and suspend it in the beer or ale, while it is working or fermenting, from two to six or eight hours, and then take it out. Wormwood ought not to lie so long, three or four hours will be quite sufficient. If the herbs are properly gathered and prepared, all their pure and balsamic virtues will readily infuse themselves into the liquor, whether wine or beer, as the pure sweet quality in malt does into the warm liquor in brewing, which is done effectually in about an hour. But if malt is suffered to remain more than six hours, before the liquor is drawn off, all the nauseous properties will be extracted, and overpower the good ones. It is the same in infusing any sort of well-prepared herbs, and great care therefore is requisite in all preparations, that the pure qualities are neither evaporated or overpowered. Otherwise, whatever it be, it will soon tend to putrefaction, and become injurious and loathsome. Beer, ale, or other liquor, into which herbs are infused, must be unadulterated, or the infusion will be destroyed by its pernicious qualities. Nothing is more prejudicial to the health, or the intellectual faculties of mankind, than adulterated liquors. Articles which in their purest state are of an equivocal character, and never to be trusted without caution, are thus converted into decided poisons.—Another way of making wormwood ale. Take a quantity of the herb, according to the intended strength of the liquor, and infuse it for half an hour in the boiling wort. Then strain it off, and set the wort to cool. Wormwood beer prepared either ways, is a fine wholesome liquor. It is gentle, warming, assisting digestion, and refining to the blood, without sending any gross fumes to the head. The same method should be observed in making all sorts of drinks, in which any strong bitter herbs are infused. It renders them pleasant and grateful, both to the stomach and palate, and preserves all the medicinal virtues. Most bitter herbs have a powerful tendency to open obstructions, if judiciously managed; but in the way in which they are too commonly made, they are not only rendered extremely unpleasant, but their medicinal properties are destroyed.

WOUNDS. If occasioned by a cut, it will be proper immediately to close the wounded part, so as to exclude the air and prevent its bleeding, and then any common sticking plaister may be applied. When the wound is deep and difficult to close, a bandage should be applied; and if the skin be lacerated, or the edges of the wound begin to be rough, lay on some lint dipped in sweet oil, and cover the whole with a piece of fine oil cloth. New honey spread on folded linen affords an excellent remedy for fresh and bleeding wounds, as it will prevent inflammation and the growth of proud flesh. In wounds which cannot readily be healed, on account of external inflammation and feverish heat, emollient poultices, composed of the crumb of bread boiled in milk, must be applied, and renewed several times in a day, without disturbing or touching the wounded part with the fingers. Wounds of the joints will heal most expeditiously by the simple application of cold water, provided the orifice of such wounds be immediately closed by means of adhesive plaster.

WOW WOW. For stewed beef, chop some parsley leaves very fine, quarter two or three pickled cucumbers or walnuts, and divide them into small squares, and set them by ready. Put into a saucepan a good bit of butter, stir up with it a table-spoonful of fine flour, and about half a pint of the broth in which the beef was boiled. Add a table-spoonful of vinegar, as much ketchup or port wine, or both, and a tea-spoonful of made mustard. Let it simmer gently till it is sufficiently thickened, put in the parsley and pickles ready prepared, and pour it over the beef, or send it up in a sauce tureen.

WRIT OF EJECTMENT. When a tenant has either received or given a proper notice to quit at a certain time, and fails to deliver up possession, it is at the option of the landlord to give notice of double rent, or issue a writ to dispossess the tenant. In the latter case he recovers the payment of the rent, or the surrender of the premises. In all cases between landlord and tenant, when half a year's rent is due, such landlord may serve a declaration or ejectment for the recovery of the premises, without any formal demand or re-entry. If the premises be unoccupied, though not surrendered, he may affix the declaration to the door, or any other conspicuous part of the dwelling, which will be deemed legal, and stand instead of a deed of re-entry.

YEAST. This is the barm or froth which rises in beer, and other malt liquors, during a state of fermentation. When thrown up by one quantity of malt or vinous liquid, it may be preserved to be put into another, at a future period; on which it will exert a similar fermentative action. Yeast is likewise used in the making of bread, without which it would be heavy and unwholesome. It has a vinous sour odour, a bitter taste arising from the hops in the malt liquor, and it reddens the vegetable blues. When it is filtered, a matter remains which possesses properties similar to vegetable gluten; by this separation the yeast loses the property of exciting fermentation, but recovers it again when the gluten is added. The addition of yeast to any vegetable substance, containing saccharine matter, excites fermentation by generating a quantity of carbonic acid gas. This very useful substance cannot always be procured conveniently from malt liquor for baking and brewing: the following method will be found useful for its extemporaneous preparation. Mix two quarts of soft water with wheat flour, to the consistence of thick gruel; boil it gently for half an hour, and when almost cold, stir into it half a pound of sugar and four spoonfuls of good yeast. Put the whole into a large jug, or earthen vessel, with a narrow top, and place it before the fire, that by a moderate heat it may ferment. The fermentation will throw up a thin liquor, which pour off and throw away; keep the remainder in a bottle, or jug tied over, and set it in a cool place. The same quantity of this as of common yeast will suffice to bake or brew with. Four spoonfuls of this yeast will make a fresh quantity as before, and the stock may always be kept up, by fermenting the new with the remainder of the former quantity.—Another method. Take six quarts of soft water, and two handfuls of wheaten meal or barley. Stir the latter in the water before the mixture is placed over the fire, where it must boil till two thirds are evaporated. When this decoction becomes cool, incorporate with it, by means of a whisk, two drams of salt of tartar, and one dram of cream of tartar, previously mixed. The whole should now be kept in a warm place. Thus a very strong yeast for brewing, distilling, and baking, may be obtained. For the last-mentioned purpose, however, it ought to be diluted with pure water, and passed through a sieve, before it is kneaded with the dough, in order to deprive it of its alkaline taste.—In countries where yeast is scarce, it is a common practice to twist hazel twigs so as to be full of chinks, and then to steep them in ale yeast during fermentation. The twigs are then hung up to dry, and at the next brewing they are put into the wort instead of yeast. In Italy the chips are frequently put into turbid wine for the purpose of clearing it, which is effected in about twenty-four hours.—A good article for baking bread may be made in the following manner. Boil a pound of fine flour, a quarter of a pound of brown sugar, and a little salt, in two gallons of water, for one hour. Let it stand till it is milk warm, then bottle and cork it close, and it will be fit for use in twenty-four hours. A pint of this yeast will make eighteen pounds of bread. Or mash a pound of mealy potatoes, and pulp them through a cullender; add two ounces of brown sugar, and two spoonfuls of common yeast. Keep it moderately warm while fermenting, and it will produce a quart of good yeast.—The best method of preserving common yeast, produced from beer or ale, is to set a quantity of it to settle, closely covered, that the spirit may not evaporate. Provide in the mean time as many small hair sieves as will hold the thick barm: small sieves are mentioned, because dividing the yeast into small quantities conduces to its preservation. Lay over each sieve a piece of coarse flannel that may reach the bottom, and leave at least eight inches over the rim. Pour off the thin liquor, and set it by to subside, as the grounds will do for immediate baking or brewing, if covered up for a few hours. Fill the sieves with the thick barm, and cover them up for two hours: then gather the flannel edges as a bag, and tie them firmly with twine. Lay each bag upon several folds of coarse linen, changing these folds every half hour, till they imbibe no more moisture. Then cover each bag with another piece of flannel, changing it if it becomes damp, and hang them in a cool airy place. The yeast should be strained before it is set to settle, and while the flannel bags are laid upon the folds of linen, they must be covered with a thick cloth. When the yeast is wanted for use, prepare a strong infusion of malt; to a gallon of which add a piece of dried barm, about the size of a goose's egg. The proportion indeed must depend upon its quality, which experience only can ascertain. The malt infusion must be nearly milk warm when the yeast is crumbled into it: for two hours it will froth high, and bake two bushels of flour into well-fermented bread. A decoction of green peas, or of ripened dry peas, with as much sugar as will sweeten it, makes fairer bread than the malt infusion; but it will take a larger quantity of dried yeast to produce fermentation. It was usual some years ago to reduce porter yeast to dryness, and in that state it was carried to the West Indies, where it was brought by means of water to its original state, and then employed as a ferment.—Another method of preserving yeast. Take a quantity of yeast, and work it well with a whisk till it becomes thin; then have a broad wooden platter, or tub, that is very clean and dry, and, with a soft brush, lay a layer of yeast all over the bottom, and turn the mouth downwards that no dust can fall in, but so that the air may come to it, to dry it. When that coat is very dry, lay on another; do so till you have as much as you intend to keep, taking care that one coat is dry before you lay on another. When you have occasion to make use of this yeast, cut a piece off, and lay it in warm water; stir it till it is dissolved, and it is fit for use. If it is for brewing, take a whisk, or a large handful of birch tied together, and dip it into the yeast, and hang it up to dry; when it is dry wrap it up in paper, and keep it in a dry place; thus you may do as many as you please. When your beer is fit to work, throw in one of your whisks, and cover it over; it will set it a working as well as fresh yeast. When you find you have a head sufficient, take out your whisk and hang it up. If the yeast is not all off, it will do for your next brewing.

YEAST CAKES. The inhabitants of Long Island in America are in the habit of making yeast cakes once a year. These are dissolved and mixed with the dough, which it raises in such a manner as to form it into very excellent bread. The following is the method in which these cakes are made. Rub three ounces of hops so as to separate them, and then put them into a gallon of boiling water, where they are to boil for half an hour. Now strain the liquor through a fine sieve into an earthen vessel, and while it is hot, put in three pounds and a half of rye flour, stirring the liquid well and quickly as the flour is put in. When it has become milk warm, add half a pint of good yeast. On the following day, while the mixture is fermenting, stir well into it seven pounds of Indian corn meal, and it will render the whole mass stiff like dough. This dough is to be well kneaded and rolled out into cakes about a third of an inch in thickness. These cakes are to be cut out into large disks or lozenges, or any other shape, by an inverted glass tumbler or any other instrument; and being placed on a sheet of tinned iron, or on a piece of board, are to be dried by the heat of the sun. If care be taken to turn them frequently, and to see that they take no wet or moisture, they will become as hard as ship biscuit, and may be kept in a bag or box, which is to be hung up or kept in an airy and perfectly dry situation. When bread is to be made, two cakes of the above-mentioned thickness, and about three inches in diameter, are to be broken and put into hot water, where they are to remain all night, the vessel standing near the fire. In the morning they will be entirely dissolved, and then the mixture is to be employed in setting the sponge, in the same way as beer yeast is used. In making a farther supply for the next year, beer or ale yeast may be used as before; but this is not necessary where a cake of the old stock remains, for this will act on the new mixture precisely in the same way. If the dry cakes were reduced to powder in a mortar, the same results would take place, with perhaps more convenience, and in less time. Indian meal is used because it is of a less adhesive nature than wheat flour, but where Indian meal cannot easily be procured, white pea-meal, or even barley-meal, will answer the purpose equally well. The principal art or requisite in making yeast cakes, consists in drying them quickly and thoroughly, and in preventing them from coming in contact with the least particle of moisture till they are used.

YEAST DUMPLINS. Make a very light dough as for bread, only in a smaller quantity. When it has been worked up, and risen a sufficient time before the fire, mould it into good sized dumplins, put them into boiling water, and let them boil twenty minutes. The dough may be made up with milk and water if preferred. These dumplins are very nice when done in a potatoe steamer, and require about thirty-five minutes, if of a good size. The steamer must not be opened till they are taken up, or it will make the dumplins heavy. Dough from the baker's will answer the purpose very well, if it cannot conveniently be made at home. The dough made for rolls is the most delicate for dumplins. If not eaten as soon as they are taken up, either out of the water or the steamer, they are apt to fall and become heavy. Eaten with cold butter they are much better than with any kind of sauce, except meat dripping directly from the pan. The addition of a few currants will make good currant dumplins.

YELLOW BLAMANGE. Pour a pint of boiling water to an ounce of isinglass, and add the peel of one lemon. When cold, put in two ounces of sifted sugar, a quarter of a pint of white wine, the yolks of four eggs, and the juice of a lemon. Stir all well together, let it boil five minutes, strain it through a bag, and put it into cups.

YELLOW DYE. There is a new stain for wood, and a yellow dye for cloth, which consists of a decoction of walnut or hickory bark, with a small quantity of alum dissolved in it, in order to give permanency to the colour. Wood of a white colour receives from the application of this liquid a beautiful yellow tinge, which is not liable to fade. It is particularly for furniture made of maple, especially that kind of it which is called bird's eye, and which is commonly prepared by scorching its surface over a quick fire. The application of the walnut dye gives a lustre even to the darkest shades, while to the paler and fainter ones it adds somewhat of a greenish hue, and to the whiter parts various tints of yellow. After applying this stain to cherry and apple wood, the wood should be slightly reddened with a tincture of some red dye, whose colour is not liable to fade. A handsome dye is thus given to it which does not hide the grain, and which becomes still more beautiful as the wood grows darker by age. Walnut bark makes the most permanent yellow dye for dyeing cloth of any of the vegetable substances used in this country. Care should be taken that the dye be not too much concentrated: when this happens, the colour is far less bright and delicate, and approaches nearer to orange. It is hardly necessary to add, that the dye should be boiled and kept in a brass vessel, or in some other which has no iron in its composition. A lively yellow colour for dyeing cloth, may be produced from potato tops. Gather them when ready to flower, press out the juice, mix it with a little water, and suffer the cloth to remain in it for twenty-four hours. The cloth, whether of wool, cotton, or flax, is then to be dipped in spring water. By plunging the cloth thus tinged with yellow, into a vessel of blue dye, a brilliant and lasting green is obtained.

YELLOW LEMON CREAM. Pare four lemons very thin into twelve large spoonfuls of water, and squeeze the juice on seven ounces of finely powdered sugar. Beat well the yolks of nine eggs; then add the peels and juice of the lemons, and work them together for some time. Strain the whole through a flannel, into a silver saucepan, or one of very nice block-tin, and set it over a gentle fire. Stir it one way till it is pretty thick, and scalding hot, but not boiling, or it will curdle. Pour it into jelly glasses. A few lumps of sugar should be rubbed hard on the lemons before they are pared, to attract the essence, and give a better colour and flavour to the cream.

YORKSHIRE CAKES. Mix two pounds of flour with four ounces of butter melted in a pint of good milk, three spoonfuls of yeast, and two eggs. Beat all well together, and let it rise; then knead it, and make it into cakes. Let them first rise on tins, and then bake in a slow oven.—Another sort is made as above, leaving out the butter. The first sort is shorter; the last lighter.

YORKSHIRE KNEAD CAKES. Rub six ounces of butter into a pound of flour till it is very fine, and mix it into a stiff paste with milk. Knead it well, and roll it out several times. Make it at last about an inch thick, and cut it into cakes, in shapes according to the fancy. Bake them on an iron girdle, and when done on one side turn them on the other. Cut them open and butter them hot. They also eat well cold or toasted. Half a pound of currants well washed and dried may be added at pleasure.

YORKSHIRE HAMS. Mix half a pound of salt, three ounces of saltpetre, half an ounce of sal prunella, and five pounds of coarse sugar. Rub the hams with this mixture, after it has been well incorporated, and lay the remainder of it upon the top. Then put some water to the pickle, adding salt till it will bear an egg. Boil and strain it, cover the hams with it, and let them lie a fortnight. Rub them well with bran, and dry them. The above ingredients are sufficient for three good hams.

YORKSHIRE PUDDING. Mix five spoonfuls of flour with a quart of milk, and three eggs well beaten. Butter the pan. When the pudding is brown by baking under the meat, turn the other side upwards, and brown that. Set it over a chafing-dish at first, and stir it some minutes. It should be made in a square pan, and cut into pieces before it comes to table.

YOUNG FOWLS. The following will be found to be a nice way of dressing up a small dish. Bone, singe, and wash a young fowl. Make a forcemeat of four ounces of veal, two ounces of lean ham scraped, two ounces of fat bacon, two hard yolks of eggs, a few sweet herbs chopped, two ounces of beef suet, a tea-spoonful of lemon peel minced fine, an anchovy, salt, pepper, and a very little cayenne. Beat all in a mortar, with a tea-cupful of crumbs, and the yolks and whites of three eggs. Stuff the inside of the fowl, draw the legs and wings inwards, tie up the neck and rump close. Stew the fowl in a white gravy; when it is done through and tender, add a large cupful of cream, with a bit of butter and flour. Give it one boil, add the squeeze of a lemon, and serve it up.

YOUNG ONION SAUCE. Peel a pint of button onions, and lay them in water. Put them into a stewpan with a quart of cold water, and let them boil for half an hour or more, till they are quite tender. They may then be put to half a pint of mushroom sauce.

FINIS.

www.ingramcontent.com/pod-product-compliance
Lightning Source LLC
Chambersburg PA
CBHW081122080526
44587CB00021B/3704